An American Movem

A Brief History of the Disciples of Christ

Winfred Ernest Garrison

Alpha Editions

This edition published in 2024

ISBN : 9789366381039

Design and Setting By
Alpha Editions
www.alphaedis.com
Email - info@alphaedis.com

As per information held with us this book is in Public Domain.
This book is a reproduction of an important historical work. Alpha Editions uses the best technology to reproduce historical work in the same manner it was first published to preserve its original nature. Any marks or number seen are left intentionally to preserve its true form.

Contents

PREFACE ....- 1 -
CHAPTER I PRELUDE ....- 3 -
CHAPTER II IDEAS WITH A HISTORY: UNION AND RESTORATION ....- 7 -
CHAPTER III THE AMERICAN SCENE ....- 17 -
CHAPTER IV THE "CHRISTIANS" ....- 26 -
CHAPTER V THE COMING OF THE CAMPBELLS ....- 39 -
CHAPTER VI WITH THE BAPTISTS, 1813-30 ....- 51 -
CHAPTER VII FIRST YEARS OF INDEPENDENCE, 1830-49 ....- 61 -
CHAPTER VIII ORGANIZATION AND TENSIONS, 1849-74 ....- 73 -
CHAPTER IX RENAISSANCE, 1874-1909 ....- 85 -
CHAPTER X GROWING INTO MATURITY, 1909-45 ....- 97 -

PREFACE

In an earlier volume, I recited the history of the Disciples of Christ under the title, *Religion Follows the Frontier*. The phrase was designed to emphasize the fact that this religious movement was born under pioneer conditions on the American frontier, in the days when the frontier was just crossing the Alleghenies, that much of its formative thinking followed patterns congenial to the frontier mind, and that its early expansion kept pace with the westward wave of migration.

Since that book is now out of print, while interest in the theme is increasing, it has seemed desirable to rewrite the history. If this were merely a sequel to the other, I would call it *Growing Up with the Country*.

It remains true that the pioneer beginnings must be remembered and understood if the initial motives and methods of the Disciples and the processes of their growth are to be understood. But important as the frontier is, as a fact in the history of the United States and of every phase of culture in the Middle West, an equally significant fact is that, as the frontier rolled westward, it left behind it a widening area in which pioneer conditions no longer prevailed. As the country was growing by the expansive drive of which the frontier was the cutting edge, it was also growing up, both behind and on the frontier. The process of maturing is as significant as that of expanding.

Since the present purpose is to survey the history of the Disciples through both of these phases, I have resisted the allurement of this second title and am giving the book a name which includes both; for the movement is distinctively American, and every American movement which began in pioneer days and has lived through the cycles of American life until now has both followed the frontier and grown up with the country.

As to the future—I am only a historian, not a prophet. But I shall be disappointed if this record of the past does not leave with the reader an acquaintance with the essential data upon which, using his own judgment and imagination, he will be disposed to project the curve of a future development far beyond any present attainments in promoting the ends for which the Disciples of Christ came into existence—the unity and purity of the Church, a reasonable and practical religion, and the enrichment of life through fellowship in the grace of our Lord Jesus Christ.

W. E. G.

CHAPTER I
PRELUDE

Who are these "Disciples of Christ"? What are these "Christian Churches" or "Churches of Christ" which now constitute one of the major religious groups in the United States? When, where, and how did they begin, and how have they become what they are?

They began early in the nineteenth century with the union of two separate movements, one of which had close kinship with two others. All four were alike in aiming to simplify the complexities of Christian faith and in going back of the creeds and the traditional practices of existing churches to the plain teaching of the New Testament. They believed that this was easy to understand, and that the divisions of Christendom would disappear if Christians would only agree to speak as the apostles spoke and to do as they did. They believed that man was sinful and needed God's salvation; but they did not believe him to be so depraved by "original sin" that he could not, by the act of his own intelligence and by his own free will, accept the means of grace that have been provided. They wanted all the churches to unite on the basis of the simple and clear requirements of discipleship as given in the New Testament, leaving all doubtful and inferential matters in the field of "opinion," in which every Christian should exercise liberty, and scrap the machinery of synods and bishops, for which they found no warrant in Scripture.

Of the two main movements, the name of Barton W. Stone was most prominent in one; the names of Thomas and Alexander Campbell in the other. Stone's movement (1804) began earlier than that of the Campbells (1809), but later than two others practically identical with it. But the Campbells' was the more dynamic, especially after it gained the advocacy of Walter Scott, who set the pattern for its evangelism. These are the four great names in the early history of the Disciples—Stone, Thomas Campbell, Alexander Campbell, and Scott. All four had been Presbyterians.

A Preview

Stone was a native American of old colonial stock, born in Maryland, educated in North Carolina after spending most of his boyhood in Virginia. He did his most important work in Kentucky. Thomas and Alexander Campbell, father and son, were born in North Ireland, were educated at Glasgow University, and came to America only a short time before the launching of their reformatory movement. The influences seen in their work are those of a British background and an American environment. The center of their activity was the southwest corner of Pennsylvania, eastern Ohio, and the narrow strip of Virginia (now West Virginia) that lies between them. Walter Scott, born in Scotland and educated in the University of Edinburgh, came to America as a young man and was a teacher in Pittsburgh when he received the impulse which led him into the Campbell movement while it was still in its initial stage.

Soon the followers of the Campbells, most of whom had recently been Baptists, and the associates of Stone, many of whom had been Presbyterians, discovered the identity of their programs, and the two movements flowed together into one. Stone's "Christians," chiefly in Kentucky and Tennessee, plus the Baptists who had joined Campbell's "Reformers" and were beginning to call themselves "Disciples," plus the hundreds of converts who had already responded to the faith-repentance-and-baptism evangelism of Scott and the others who had learned to preach as he did, added up to twenty or thirty thousand by the time of this union in 1832. From that point, growth was rapid, by persistent and persuasive preaching, by propaganda in print, and by the constant movement of population to new frontiers farther and farther west carrying with it the nuclei of new churches in the new settlements.

This was at first a popular movement, unorganized and uncontrolled, with no high command, no common treasury, no general machinery for either promotion or direction. But the increasing magnitude of the enterprise, the changing social conditions as the Middle West grew out of its frontier stage, and the realization that such a religious body as this was coming to be had some responsibilities other than propagating itself—all these things made organization inevitable. Then followed colleges, missionary societies, conventions, and the other apparatus of an organic fellowship. But still, and always, there was fierce resistance to anything that seemed to threaten encroachment upon the liberty of the Christian individual or of the local congregation. Cooperation must always be voluntary.

So the Disciples of Christ have become "a great people." It is to their credit that there has always been some confusion about their name. Aiming to promote union, they wanted a scriptural name that all Christians might use. They found in the New Testament certain terms applied to the undivided church or to its members. Alexander Campbell liked the name "Disciples." Stone preferred "Christians." A local church is commonly called a "Christian Church," or a "Church of Christ"; less frequently a "Church of Disciples of Christ." The name "Churches of Christ" (in the plural), as the designation for a group, generally refers to the conservative or antimissionary-society churches which became completely separated from the main body in 1906.

But, though it is well to have unsectarian names which any Christian or any Christian church can use, it is highly convenient to have some designation which others do not generally use, so that the public will know what is meant when reference is made to the churches or members of this movement. Its objective may be the unity of all Christ's followers, but meanwhile it is a specific group, if not a denomination then a "brotherhood"—and a brotherhood is just as distinct an entity as a denomination. So, as a term that will be generally understood to mean *us*, the term "Disciples of Christ" has come into common use.

THREE SOURCES, TWO STREAMS

Looking back from a later time to describe the reformatory movement as it had been in the 1820's, Walter Scott wrote that there were then "three parties struggling to restore original Christianity."

The *first* of these was the independent "Churches of Christ," which stemmed from the work of Glas, Sandeman, the Haldane brothers, and similar eighteenth century British restorers of primitive Christianity. Scott himself for a time belonged to one of these churches in Pittsburgh. They were few in number, had little relation to each other, little concern for union, and no evangelistic drive. This party is important for our purpose because it is one of the sources from which the Campbells derived suggestions for a rational conception of faith and the idea of "restoration" in its more legalistic and literalistic aspects. It will be described more particularly in the latter part of Chapter II.

The *second* was the "Christian" churches, existing in three independent groups in Virginia and North Carolina, in New England, New York, and Pennsylvania, and in Kentucky and adjacent states. The last of these divisions is doubtless the one Scott had chiefly in mind, and it is the one most closely related to our theme. Some account of these three bodies of "Christians" will be given in Chapter IV.

The *third*, said Scott, "originating with the writings and labors of Bro. A. Campbell," was at that time "chiefly in the bosom of the Regular Baptist churches." Chapters V and VI will tell the story of these "Reformers" down to the time of their separation from the Baptists.

The first of these is significant as an influence and as part of the historical background. It contributed to the united movement few churches, few men, and no literature; but two of the men who came to the Disciples through this channel were invaluable—Walter Scott and Isaac Errett. The other two parties became substantial bodies, and they are the two main streams whose confluence produced the Disciples of Christ.

CHAPTER II
IDEAS WITH A HISTORY: UNION AND RESTORATION

The union of all Christians and the restoration of primitive Christianity were the two main ideas announced by Thomas Campbell in his *Declaration and Address* in 1809 and championed by Alexander Campbell for fifty years thereafter. With some differences of emphasis and phrasing, they were the ruling ideas of Stone and the other reformers whose work preceded, paralleled, and reinforced his. To this day, these are the two foci of interest among Disciples, and every difference of opinion which threatens to create parties among them revolves about answers to the questions: "Restoration of what?" and "What price union?"

Each of these ideas, union and restoration, has a long history, only a small part of which can be told here, but part of which must be told.

THE IDEA OF UNION

The essential unity of the church was and is a basic principle of Roman Catholicism. It was a formative idea in the Catholic Church of the second and third centuries, which had not yet become Roman, and it continued to be so through all the history of the imperial church of the Middle Ages. The great Protestant reformers of the sixteenth century did not cease to be "catholic" in their belief that the church was divinely intended to be one body. They wanted to reform the church, not to break it into pieces. Efforts to heal the breach with Rome were long continued and frequently renewed. But reunion with Rome proved to be impossible on any other terms than submission to that usurped authority from which they had revolted. Different types of Protestantism soon appeared. The principal varieties—Lutheranism, Calvinism, Zwinglianism, Anabaptism, episcopal Anglicanism—represented, not divisions of an originally united Protestantism, but separate and independent revolts from Rome. Among these there was a long series of conferences, negotiations, and proposals designed to unite, if possible, all Protestants into one body. Such efforts continued to be made throughout the seventeenth century.

In the sixteenth and seventeenth centuries, most people believed that a nation could not be politically united unless it had only one church, of which all its people were members. Consequently, the power of the state was generally used to support one church and to suppress all others. "Dissenters" were subjected to various degrees of pressure or restraint to induce them to conform to the established church. Only gradually did dissenters gain liberty of conscience. The intolerance and persecution of which they were the victims meanwhile proved the importance that was attached to the unity of the church, at least within the limits of each nation. This kind of unity without liberty, or compulsory religious unity conceived as an instrument of social control and as essential to political stability, was the expression of a social philosophy which was carried over from medieval Roman Catholic Europe to the modern European nations, both Catholic and Protestant. The idea of unity as an important characteristic of the church did not need to be invented or even discovered in modern times. It was there all the while. But it needed to be liberated from its political entanglements, as the church itself did. It needed to be conceived in terms consistent with the spiritual nature of the church and the civil rights of man. Both the church and the citizen had to be made free.

Besides the efforts of politicians and ecclesiastics in established churches to get church unity by compulsion, there were a few churchmen and independent thinkers who argued that unity might be attained by requiring agreement only upon the few saving essentials of Christianity and leaving everyone free to hold his own opinions on all the doubtful and disputatious matters of doctrine, polity, and ritual. Thus the Puritan Stillingfleet wrote in his *Eirenicon* (1662):

> It would bee strange the Church should require more than Christ himself did, and make other conditions of her communion than our Savior did of Discipleship.... Without all controversie, the main in-let of all the distractions, confusions and divisions of the Christian world hath been by adding other conditions of Church-communion than Christ hath done.

In very similar words, and only a few years later, the English philosopher John Locke argued that, since men differ in their interpretations of the Bible and always will, none should seek to impose his opinions on another, and that their differences should not divide them. In his first *Letter Concerning Toleration* (1689), Locke wrote:

Since men are so solicitous about the true church, I would only ask them here by the way, if it be not more agreeable to the Church of Christ to make the conditions of her communion consist in such things, and such things only, as the Holy Spirit has in the Holy Scriptures declared, in express words, to be necessary to salvation?

And Rupertius Meldenius made the classic statement of this principle when he said: "In essentials, unity; in non-essentials, liberty; in all things, charity."

But the churches did not respond to this appeal for liberty of opinion within the church that there might be union of Christians in one church. Slowly, however, the governments of most European countries in which the Roman Catholic Church did not exercise control yielded to the demand for liberty of religious opinion within the state. With this grant of toleration to churches which were mutually intolerant, the states preserved their unity, while the church sank into a condition of complacent sectarianism. During the seventeenth century there had been many pleas for church unity through liberty. The eighteenth century thought much about liberty and little about unity. But it is to be remembered that, when a new call to unity was sounded in America at the beginning of the nineteenth century, it was the renewal of a campaign that already had a long history. It came at a time when the churches in America, happy in the complete liberty they enjoyed and in their freedom from state control and equality before the law, had ceased to be much concerned about unity and had settled into the conviction that division and denominationalism represented the normal condition of the church.

THE IDEA OF RESTORATION

The other principle stressed by "the reformation of the nineteenth century" was the restoration of primitive Christianity. That also had a long history, which can be only sketched. Thomas and Alexander Campbell made a new use of this idea, and it will have a large place in the story of their work, but in order to understand their contribution it is necessary to note that the idea itself was not new. The oldest Christian bodies claim to have preserved primitive Christianity uncorrupted, and every reforming movement in the history of the church has claimed in some sense to offer a restoration of its pristine purity. A few citations, among many that might be offered, will make this clear.

The Roman Catholic Church professes to present original Christianity unchanged. "What Christ made it in the beginning, that must it ever remain," says Rev. B. J. Otten, S.J., in *The Catholic Church and Modern Christianity*. A representative of the Eastern Orthodox Church more recently wrote: "The Russian Church, having alone preserved the picture of Christ, must restore that picture to Europe." A Chinese Nestorian who visited Europe in the thirteenth century said to the College of Cardinals: "As for us Orientals, the Holy Apostles taught us, and up to the present we hold fast to what they have committed to us."

The great reformers of the sixteenth century conceived of their work as clearing away the human additions and getting back to primitive Christianity as found in the Bible. Luther, Zwingli, and Calvin all made their appeal directly to Scripture. Bucer exhorted believers to "reject all false speculations and all human opinions." The Anabaptists cited the example of the first Christians as their authority for refusing to have a creed or to bear arms or to take oaths or to hold civil office, and Melchior Hofmann announced a "resurrection of primitive Christianity." When Queen Elizabeth was masquerading as a Lutheran, for diplomatic reasons, she said she would hold to the Augsburg Confession because it "conformed most closely to the faith of the early church." Chillingworth stated the principle of the Reformation in the words, "The Bible and the Bible alone is the religion of Protestants," excluding ecclesiastical tradition because it furnished neither legitimate additions to the primitive faith and practice nor trustworthy evidence as to what these had been. Episcopalians, Presbyterians, and Congregationalists, in seventeenth-century England, all claimed the authority and example of the New Testament church in support of their respective forms of church organization and their conceptions of the ministry.

One modern Lutheran writer declares that "the Lutheran Church is the old original church," and another that "Lutheranism is Bible Christianity." A book issued by the Presbyterian Board of Publication says that "of all the churches now existing in the world, the Presbyterian Church comes nearest to the apostolic model." John Wesley wrote to the Methodists in America after the Revolution that, being free from the English state and hierarchy, they "are now at full liberty to follow the Scriptures and the primitive church."

More secular thinkers have made similar appeal to the ancient standards as the cure for the modern church's ills. Rousseau "only wanted to simplify Christianity and bring it back to its origins," says A. Aulard in his work on *Christianity and the French Revolution*. John Adams wrote in 1770: "Where do we find a precept in the Gospel requiring ecclesiastical synods, councils, creeds, oaths, subscriptions, and whole cart-loads of other trumpery that we find religion encumbered with in these days?"

These references do not, of course, prove that all or any of those who claimed to follow the primitive model actually did so. The point is that they claimed to do it. The restoration of primitive purity has been the standard formula for reformation.

EIGHTEENTH CENTURY RESTORATIONISTS

In the eighteenth century there arose, in Great Britain, some movements which applied the restoration formula in a way that contributed more directly to the Campbells' use of it than those already mentioned. None of these gained a large following, and even their names have been forgotten by all except special students of the period. Their leaders were bold and independent spirits who saw that the church needed reforming and were not afraid to attempt it. They laid hold of a great idea, but they were never able to build a substantial enterprise upon it. Yet they handed it down to those who could.

John Glas, a minister of the Church of Scotland, about 1727 came to the conviction that, since the New Testament church had no connection with the state, the whole scheme of establishment as embodied in the "National Covenant" was without authority. Further, he found no warrant for synods or other law-making bodies with power to fix standards of doctrine for the whole church and exercise discipline over it. He therefore left the state church and organized an independent congregation. He next inquired how this autonomous local church should order its affairs, conduct its worship, and establish its ministry. Finding that the New Testament churches "came together on the first day of the week to break bread," whereas the Presbyterian Church of Scotland observed the Lord's Supper no oftener than once a month, Glas and his associates adopted the practice of weekly communion. "They agreed that in this, as in everything else," says his biographer, "they ought to be followers of the first Christians, being guided and directed by the Scriptures alone."

Further, Glas found that in the early churches there was a "plurality of elders" and that "mutual edification" was practiced—that is, that public services of worship were not conducted solely by one ordained minister. This opened the way for a large degree of lay leadership and less emphasis on the special functions of the clergy. After it was observed that the Epistles of Paul made no mention of a university education or a knowledge of the ancient languages among the qualifications for the eldership, the line between clergy and laity grew still more dim.

Robert Sandeman, who married one of Glas's daughters, adopted his principles and gave them a somewhat more vigorous advocacy, so that the resulting churches were more often called "Sandemanian" than "Glasite." Through their combined efforts, there came into existence a few small churches, probably never more than a dozen or two, in various parts of Scotland and England. Michael Faraday, the famous chemist, was a member of a Sandemanian church in London. Apparently not more than six or eight such churches were organized in America, and not all these were known by that name or acknowledged any special connection with Glas or Sandeman. Their basic theory led them to "call no man master" and to exercise their liberty in deciding, from their own study of Scripture, what should be their faith and practice. Robert Sandeman spent his last years in Danbury, Connecticut, where he died in 1771, after organizing a church there. There were Sandemanian churches in Boston. All of them in this country, so far as known, were in New England.

Glas and Sandeman did not find that the New Testament churches practiced only the immersion of believers as baptism. But some of their associates in Scotland did. Archibald McLean was the leader of these. They came to be called "Old Scotch Baptists." In coming to this position they seem not to have been influenced by the English Baptists but were moved by their own independent study of the New Testament. Similarly, some of the members of Sandeman's church in Danbury later reached the same conviction, withdrew, and formed an immersionist "Church of Christ."

Although the Sandemanians remained few and inconspicuous, Robert Sandeman himself was a theological thinker of great ability and clarity. His writings were widely read and highly regarded by many who had no affiliation with his movement and who did not share his views about the importance of reproducing exactly the model of the primitive church. This was especially true of his treatises dealing with the nature of faith and with the priority of faith to repentance. If this now seems a dry and technical matter, it did not seem so then and it had very practical implications. The gist of his thought on this point was that it is within the power of every man to believe the gospel and obey its commands to his own salvation. The more popular theory among eighteenth-century evangelicals was that sinful and "fallen" man has no power to believe. He can repent and "mourn" for the sinful state which he inherited from Adam, but then he must wait for a special and miraculous act of enabling grace to give him faith. This gift of faith and regeneration will be certified to him by an exalted state of feeling which constitutes his religious experience and is the evidence of his "acceptance with God."

Against this, Sandeman put the doctrine that God had not only revealed his truth in terms intelligible to man and provided the means of salvation through Christ, but had also furnished in Scripture adequate evidence of the truth of his revelation, so that the natural man, just as he is, with all his sins, can weigh the evidence and accept the truth. That acceptance is faith. Saving faith, said Sandeman, is an act of man's reason, and it differs from any other act of belief only in being belief of a saving fact.

This view of faith came to have immense importance in the history of the Disciples. They developed from it, as Sandeman did not, the method of a very successful evangelism. There were other influences besides that of Sandeman which led Alexander Campbell to this view, especially the philosophy of John Locke and, above all, his own study of the New Testament. But it is known that he had read Sandeman's writings carefully in his youth and regarded them highly, and the similarity of his view to Sandeman's on this point cannot be regarded as purely coincidental. A Baptist writer later tried to prove that the Disciples were "an offshoot of Sandemanianism." (Whitsitt: *The Origin of the Disciples of Christ*, 1888.) "Offshoot" is the wrong word; a mighty river is not an offshoot from a tiny trickle. But there was undoubtedly an influence: first, in the emphasis upon restoring the procedure of the primitive church; second, in the conception of faith as intelligent belief based on evidence.

RESTORATION AND DIVISION

Two wealthy brothers, Robert and James Alexander Haldane, laymen of the Church of Scotland, became alarmed at the state of religion in their country. It seemed to them that the church had become merely a respectable institution enjoying the patronage of the state, supporting a clergy chiefly concerned about their own professional dignity and privileges, and doing little to carry a vital gospel to those who needed it most. At their own expense, while still members of the Church of Scotland, they attempted to start a mission to India (which was frustrated by the East India Company), brought twenty-four native children from Africa to be educated in England and sent back to evangelize their own people (but the Anglican Church took them over), built tabernacles for evangelistic meetings, sent agents through Scotland to organize Sunday schools, and established institutes for the training of lay preachers. Beginning with no very definite theology or theory about the church, they gradually came to the belief that the chief trouble with the church was its departure from the primitive pattern as described in the New Testament.

In 1799 the Haldane brothers withdrew from the Church of Scotland and organized an independent church in Edinburgh. Acting on the advice of Greville Ewing, a minister who was in charge of their training school in Glasgow, they adopted the congregational form of organization and the weekly communion as being in accordance with the usage of the apostolic churches. Soon they became earnest advocates of the restoration of primitive Christianity by following in all respects the pattern of the New Testament churches. J. A. Haldane published, in 1805, a book entitled, *A View of the Social Worship and Ordinances of the First Christians, Drawn from the Scriptures alone; Being an Attempt to Enforce their Divine Obligation, and to Represent the Guilty and Evil Consequences of Neglecting them.* This book contains an argument for infant baptism on the ground that it was the apostolic practice, but two years later the Haldanes decided that the evidence of Scripture was against this position, so they gave it up and were immersed.

Other Haldanean churches sprang up, both in Great Britain and in America. There were never many of them. No organization bound them together, they had no cooperative work, and they took no distinctive name. But they swelled the number of those scattered and independent "Churches of Christ" which were attempting, with somewhat differing results, to restore the primitive order. The tendency of all these churches was toward a rather literalistic and legalistic interpretation of Scripture, with special emphasis upon exact conformity to a pattern of ordinances, organization, and worship. A few years later, two of these churches, one in Edinburgh and the other in New York, engaged in an earnest but very courteous argument by correspondence as to whether the New Testament commanded that the worship service be opened with a hymn or with a prayer. Each quoted what seemed relevant and convincing texts: "First of all giving thanks" meant prayer first; "Enter into his courts with praise" meant hymn first.

The Sandemanian churches also, in their anxiety to do everything exactly as the first churches had done, took as binding commands for all time many texts generally considered mere descriptions of customs of the first century or instructions suitable to that time. Thus they "saluted one another with a holy kiss" (Romans 16:16); considered private wealth sinful (Acts 2:44, 45), though they did not actually practice community of goods; made a weekly collection for the poor (1 Cor. 16:2); partook of a common meal in connection with the Lord's Supper (Acts 2:46); and for a time practiced foot washing (John 13:14). They practiced close communion even to the extent of excluding those of their own number who opposed infant baptism.

None of these churches—Sandemanian, Haldanean and other—showed any special interest in Christian unity. Indeed, there was not much division in Scotland, where they originated, for almost everybody was Presbyterian. The restoration of primitive Christianity was, for them, a movement not toward unity but away from it. They were little interested in being united with other Christians, but were anxious to be *right*, let who would be wrong. Their insistence upon conformity to an exact pattern of supposedly primitive procedure, about which there were sure to be differences of opinion, tended toward division. This was doubtless one reason why their success was so small.

Many other small and independent groups of restorers of primitive Christianity arose in Great Britain in the eighteenth century and the first years of the nineteenth. One writer claims to have listed forty, but the present author has not been able to find so many. They adopted names of confusing similarity, either "Church of Christ" or some name of which "Brethren" formed a part. They came and went, united and divided. Though most of the groups disappeared, the type persisted. It is now represented at its best, and with important modifications and additions, in the British "Churches of Christ" which are in communion with the Disciples of Christ in America.

For three hundred years Protestantism had been based on the idea that the Scriptures were the only guide, and the restoration of the essential features of primitive Christianity the only method, for reforming the church. In the sixteenth century, after freedom from the Roman hierarchy and from bondage to ecclesiastical tradition had been won, the effort was chiefly to restore the pure doctrine of the apostles. In the seventeenth, attention was given to restoring a divinely authorized form of church polity, which some held to be episcopal, others presbyterial, others congregational. When the major divisions of Protestantism had crystallized around their respective bodies of doctrine and systems of polity, the restoration concept passed out of their minds. It was taken up by smaller groups of dissenters and irregulars who, in the eighteenth century, scarcely noticed by the larger bodies, bent their energies to restoring the ordinances and worship of the church, as well as its structure, according to what they conceived to be the original pattern.

When Thomas and Alexander Campbell adopted the familiar formula of restoration and combined it with a plea for union, they gave it a different application and produced a strikingly different result.

CHAPTER III
THE AMERICAN SCENE

Three things must be noted as characteristic of America in the period which witnessed the beginnings of the Disciples of Christ. First, this was a very young nation. Its population was small. Its frontier, which began even east of the Allegheny Mountains, was sparsely settled, but settlers were pouring into it rapidly. The Disciples began on the frontier and moved westward with it. Second, the country's religious forces were divided into five or six large sects of approximately equal size and many more small ones. The members of all these together constituted only a small fraction, perhaps 10 per cent, of the total population. In no other country was so large a proportion of the people religiously unattached. Third, America had a kind and a degree of religious liberty which had never before existed anywhere in Christendom. Church and state were separated; the support of the churches was purely voluntary; no church had legal advantage or social pre-eminence over others; and every man had complete liberty to adopt any form of worship and belief he thought right (or none), to propagate his faith without hindrance, or to start a new religious organization if he so desired. This combination of circumstances had never before existed. These factors in the environment are immensely important for our study.

Since the movements which produced the Disciples of Christ began so near the beginning of the nineteenth century, we may take the year 1800 as a suitable point at which to make a cross section of the United States and observe, in a very general way, the state of the nation.

AMERICA IN 1800

George Washington had died the year before. John Adams was president. The country consisted of sixteen states, only Vermont, Kentucky, and Tennessee having been added to the original thirteen. It had a population of 5,308,483, less than 10 per cent of whom lived west of the Alleghenies. (Twenty years later, in spite of the great westward movement, 73 per cent of the people were still on the Atlantic slope.) The population, wealth, industries, and cultural institutions were very largely concentrated not only east of the mountains but in the eastern part of the area east of the mountains. The Atlantic tidewater belt, from Boston to Charleston, contained the great preponderance of everything that made this a nation—except its land, its undeveloped resources, and its pioneering spirit. But the eastern cities that loom so large in history were still small: Philadelphia, 28,522; Boston, 24,037; New York, with 60,515 within the boundaries of present-day Manhattan, had already taken first place. In the summer of 1800 the seat of the national government was moved from Philadelphia to the unfinished buildings in the almost uninhabited area that was to become the city of Washington.

The vast region now occupied by the five populous states west of the Alleghenies and north of the Ohio River had a grand total of 51,000 inhabitants. It had been organized as the Northwest Territory under the Ordinance of 1787, and the Indians had been moved out of the eastern and southern parts of it in 1795 under a treaty forced upon them after Anthony Wayne's expedition against them. Pittsburgh was a town of 1,565, the head of navigation on the Ohio. In 1803 the state of Ohio was carved out of the Northwest Territory. By 1830 it had a population of more than 900,000. So urgent was the drive toward the open frontier and so rapid the development of its communities that, while trying to realize the newness and emptiness of the region at a given period, one must be on guard against failing to realize the rate of change. Moreover, some parts of the area were much more advanced than others.

Kentucky was about a generation ahead of the adjacent Northwest Territory in settlement and culture. It had a college, the first west of the mountains, even before it got statehood in 1792. By 1800 it had a population of 220,000. Lexington, a town of 1,797 (including 439 slaves), its metropolis, the seat of the college, and the social and economic center of the Bluegrass Region, could make a plausible claim to the title, "the Athens of the West." The churches came to Kentucky, as they did everywhere, with the first wave of settlers. By 1800 the Presbyterians had a synod and several presbyteries. The most numerous body was the Baptists, who reported 106 churches with 5,000 members. The Methodists, with perhaps half that number in the state, organized a Western Conference the next year, composed of circuits in Kentucky, Tennessee, and the Northwest Territory. These were the three vigorous and aggressive churches on the frontier.

The Mississippi River was the western boundary of the United States (until 1803), and Florida was still a Spanish possession.

Louisiana Territory and Florida were both held by Roman Catholic powers, and Protestant churches were not permitted.

AMERICAN CHURCHES IN 1800

The term, "the Church," had little meaning in America at and after the beginning of the federal period. There was no *Church*, either as a visible and functioning reality or as an ideal; there were only *churches*. If we call them "sects," it is not to criticize but simply to describe the fact that the church had been *cut* into many parts. In view of the kind of compulsory unity (or attempted unity) in European and British Christianity out of which these sects arose, the divisions were not to their discredit. Sectarianism was a stage through which Christianity had to pass on the road to freedom and unity. But the fact of division is the one now before us.

The largest denominations were the Congregational, Episcopal, Presbyterian, Baptist, and Methodist. There were also important bodies of Dutch Reformed, German Reformed, French Huguenots, Lutherans, Quakers, and Roman Catholics, and such smaller groups as the Moravians, Mennonites, Dunkers, Schwenkfelders, and the Ephrata Society.

The original settlement of the first Atlantic Seaboard colonies, especially Virginia and New England, combined the religious with the economic motive. Even the nationalistic impulse to extend British power was as much religious as political, for it included zeal for the extension of Protestantism on a scale to match and check the Spanish Roman Catholic empire which already included Florida, the West Indies, Mexico, and most of South America.

Virginia was Anglican by intention, but from the start the Puritan element in both the company and the colony was strong. When the first settlement was made, and for a good while after, the Puritans were still a party in the Church of England. Episcopacy remained established in Virginia until the Revolution, though there was a strong influx of Scotch-Irish (Presbyterian, of course) and of Baptists in the eighteenth century. Since there was no Anglican bishop in America during all these years, there could be no confirmations. As always with established churches, nominal adherents greatly outnumbered communicants, and many were content with a "gentlemanly conformity." Episcopacy was established also in North and South Carolina, though it never had a majority in either colony, and in New York after the British took it from the Dutch in 1667.

The great Puritan migration to New England had for its religious purpose the founding of a Puritan state somewhat on the pattern of Calvin's Geneva. The developments of the seventeenth and eighteenth centuries produced, instead, a group of colonies—states in the American union by 1800—in which Congregationalism was the "standing order," or established church, and one state, Rhode Island, in which, thanks to Roger Williams and the Baptists, complete religious liberty, deliberately adopted as a matter of conviction, got its first fair trial as a principle of government. But Congregationalism, though clinging to some of its legal advantages, had also grown tolerant, partly because dissenters and noncommunicants had become so very numerous. As early as 1760, the president of Yale estimated that 12 per cent in the four New England colonies were dissenters, and that not more than one-fifth of the others were communicant members of Congregational churches.

New England Congregationalism, though already disturbed by the theological controversy which later produced the Unitarian defection, was in the main soundly Calvinistic. It differed from Presbyterianism only in its tradition of the independence of the local church, and even this was qualified by the growth of what was called "associationism" by those who viewed it with alarm. So, when an interest in home missions began to appear, about 1800, the Plan of Union was formed under which Congregationalists and Presbyterians cooperated until 1837 in carrying the gospel to the new settlements, first in western New York and then in the regions beyond. The Presbyterians ultimately got most of the churches organized in the Middle West by Congregational missionaries operating under this plan.

Presbyterians came from England, Scotland, and North Ireland. They never had a colony of their own, though they missed having Massachusetts Bay only because the Presbyterian Puritans who founded it became Congregational. Puritans who came to other colonies generally were and remained Presbyterians. They found a footing in New York, New Jersey, Maryland, Virginia, the Carolinas, and Georgia and were among the first settlers of Kentucky. Pennsylvania became the scene of some of their most vigorous activities, both in and around Philadelphia and in the central and western part, where they were the most numerous and influential group. William Tennent's "Log College" at Neshaminy (1720) initiated theological education in America, at least outside of Harvard's effort to provide a learned clergy for New England.

It trained evangelists as well as scholars, and led to the founding of Princeton. The great Scotch-Irish immigration, about the middle of the eighteenth century, brought both regular Presbyterians, in communion with the Church of Scotland, and Seceder Presbyterians, representing the Great Secession of 1733. Large numbers of both came to the western parts of Pennsylvania and Virginia, where these Presbyterian Ulstermen "formed an American Ulster larger and richer than that they had abandoned," as one of them wrote, with some exaggeration of the degree of their occupancy though not of the size and resources of the area. Thomas Campbell was following a stream of Scotch-Irish Seceder Presbyterians when he migrated from the vicinity of Belfast, Ireland, to the southwestern corner of Pennsylvania.

Baptist beginnings in America are easily localized in Rhode Island, but their dispersal and multiplication cannot be simply diagramed. They went everywhere, on their individual initiative, with no general organization, were persecuted wherever intolerance ruled, and generally despised by their more conventional and respectable neighbors, chiefly because they insisted that religion was a purely voluntary matter, that Christian, Turk, Jew, or atheist should be allowed to follow his own convictions about faith and worship, and that the state had nothing to do with it. That position seemed almost equivalent to anarchy. The fact that most of the Baptist preachers were ignorant men, or self-taught and uncouth, and that a great many of them were farmers six days in the week and preachers only on Sunday, made the matter worse. But the Baptists did have a college, founded in 1764, which became Brown University. In cities and towns their preachers became more urbane, but they kept the aggressiveness and the popular appeal which brought immense success to their cause in the Middle West and in the South. Regular Baptists were Calvinistic. Their Philadelphia Confession, which was very similar in doctrine to the Presbyterians' Westminster Confession, was commonly used as a standard of orthodoxy. It taught that Christ died only for the elect. But there were also "General Baptists," who believed in a general atonement, or that Christ died for all. The difference between the two became significant.

Methodism in America began when two or three lay preachers came in the 1760's, and when John Wesley sent two preachers from England in 1769. But the revival of 1740, known as the Great Awakening, had prepared the way for it. Through the Revolution and until 1784, Methodism remained nominally a movement in the Anglican Church, but it had its societies, preachers, classes, and circuits, and its evangelists converted thousands of the religiously indifferent. Formal organization began with the Christmas conference, 1784. The Methodist system of supervision by "superintendents," who promptly became bishops, and by presiding elders, with preachers riding circuits and class leaders conserving local gains, constituted a planned economy in the business of serving the religious needs of the frontier. But without tireless energy and zealous devotion, all this machinery could not have been effective. Methodism began on the Atlantic Seaboard and it had good success there, but the scene of its most spectacular growth was in the West and South. By 1800 the Methodists, Baptists, and Presbyterians had become the great "popular churches" on the frontier; and the frontier itself was on the verge of a startlingly rapid transformation.

It must not be supposed that the attitudes of the denominations toward each other were altogether those of mutual hostility and competition, or even of isolation. There was much of this, but there was also much of mutual respect and friendliness. From 1800 to about 1837 there was a noticeable increase of cooperation among the members of many denominations. This is seen in the earliest phases of Sunday school work, in Bible publication and distribution, in certain aspects of foreign and home missionary activity, and in the antislavery and temperance societies. But the most conspicuous feature of American Christianity continued to be its divided state.

LAND OF THE FREE

One reason for this sectarian condition was that this was a free country. Under the First Amendment to the Constitution, which is the first article of the Bill of Rights, no church could ever receive special favors from the government nor could there be discrimination against any. When the American Government adopted this hands-off policy, leaving the whole matter of religion to the churches and to the people, the old compulsory unity disappeared—even the ghost of unity which England had, with its one national church and a number of "dissenting" bodies still under certain legal handicaps.

It is little wonder that America had many churches. Colonists had come from many countries bringing all the varieties of religion that existed in all those countries. Many of them had come as refugees from persecution. In later years, some divisions occurred on American soil, but the sects that were here in 1800 had all been imported from Europe.

Moreover, since the United States was formed by the union of thirteen colonies, the new nation, of course, had as many different churches as all the colonies together had had. In some colonies, especially Rhode Island, Pennsylvania, and Delaware, there had been a considerable variety of churches enjoying equal liberty. In others the situation was much as it was in England at the same time, with their established churches and with dissenting bodies existing as best they could under the shadow of the favored church. The founders and builders of the American colonies, with a few exceptions, had not believed in the separation of church and state or in equal liberty for all religious groups. But the idea of religious liberty had been growing, and the multiplicity of churches in the new nation made the establishment of any one of them as *the* national church a practical impossibility. No one even suggested it in the Constitutional Convention of 1787.

It is hard for us now to realize how continuous and almost universal had been the belief that the welfare of the state was bound up with religious uniformity. For more than a thousand years, and throughout Christendom, practically everybody except little bands of heretics and rebels believed that the institutional unity of the church was essential to the security of the state and the stability of the social order, and that it was the state's duty to enforce this unity. That belief furnished the reason—and when not the reason, the excuse—for most of the persecutions that have occurred. Roman Catholics, of course, believed it, and it is still the official teaching of the Roman Catholic Church. But most Protestants also believed it. Only the Baptists and Quakers and some small separatist sects in Germany believed in religious liberty as a matter of principle. But the established and respectable bodies considered these as wild-eyed radicals.

Episcopalians and Puritans who founded colonies in America brought with them this idea of a state church and a religious unity enforced by the police power, not because they were bigoted or cruel by preference but because they believed, as almost everybody had believed for centuries, that in no other way could a political society be strong enough to survive. Surprise is sometimes expressed at the "inconsistency" of the Puritans, who "came seeking religious liberty" and then persecuted the Quakers and Baptists. But there is no inconsistency, for they did not come seeking religious liberty. They came to establish a Puritan state.

They had to learn religious liberty after they arrived, and they were rather slow in learning it. But even the vestiges of the colonial religious establishments withered away after the Revolution, and America became, in fact as well as in constitutional theory, a nation in which all churches, like all individuals, are free and equal before the law.

A new epoch in the history of religion began when a nation was born which (*a*) disclaimed for its civil power the right and duty of giving special protection to a favored church, (*b*) declared implicitly, as the Virginia Bill of Rights in 1776 had done explicitly, that religion must be purely voluntary, and (*c*) abandoned the medieval political philosophy which justified intolerance on the theory that the state must enforce religious uniformity in the interest of its own stability and security.

These new American conditions had, among others, three results that are of vital importance in connection with the present study:

First, the removal of the repressive hand of government made it easier for new religious movements to spring up or for old ones to divide. Hence new divisions in the church arose in addition to those which had been imported from Europe. The divided state of the Christian forces became more acute and called more urgently for correction.

Second, the problem of Christian union ceased to be in any sense a political problem and became a purely religious problem to be solved by religious means. Seventeenth century advocates of union had, to be sure, preached brotherly love and made some statements about uniting on the simple essentials of Christianity; but they had sought support largely from political leaders, trying to show them how a national church, united by making concessions to bring back the dissenters, would increase the nation's strength, or how an alliance between the churches of different countries would be a good stroke of diplomacy. The conceptions of complete religious liberty for the individual and of free churches in a free state introduced an entirely new approach to the question of union. Those conceptions had to be thoroughly worked out before the problem of Christian union in the modern sense—which is also the primitive sense—could even be stated; and they had to be made operative in government before a solution could be hopefully attempted. There had to be complete freedom to divide before there could be a union that would not deny freedom.

Third, separation of church and state and recognition of the voluntary character of religion threw directly upon the members of churches the whole responsibility for supporting the churches and promoting their work by voluntary contributions. The Christian discovery and conquest of America was to be organized and financed on a voluntary basis.

Such, in bare outline, was the American scene in which the forerunners and fathers of the Disciples of Christ, about the beginning of the nineteenth century, began to advocate a simple and noncreedal Christianity, the union of all Christians on the basis of the essential and primitive conditions of discipleship, and the restoration of such features of the "ancient order of things" as might be agreed upon as designed to be permanent practices of the church.

CHAPTER IV
THE "CHRISTIANS"

The longest direct tributary to the stream which became the Disciples of Christ is the movement with which the name of Barton W. Stone is generally associated. This took visible form when he and his four colleagues dissolved the Springfield Presbytery, in 1804, and took the name "Christians." Back of this, however, lay two other movements which led to the formation of "Christian" churches. Stone was certainly fully informed about the first of these before taking his own step, but probably not about the second. The three were so nearly identical in principles and objectives that they considered themselves as constituting a single body as soon as they learned of one another's work and long before they had any organizational unity. We shall consider the three parts of the "Christian" Church in the order of their origin. The first was a secession from the Methodists, the second from the Baptists, the third from the Presbyterians.

IN VIRGINIA AND NORTH CAROLINA, 1794

Methodism was not a denomination but only a revival movement in the Church of England until the end of the Revolutionary War. In 1771, John Wesley sent Francis Asbury from England. He became the most important factor in winning converts, enlisting workers, setting up the system of circuits and itinerant preachers, and organizing the church. By 1784, about 15,000 members were enrolled in Methodist societies in Virginia and the adjacent states. But these societies were not churches. They had no ordained ministers and therefore could not have the sacraments. Asbury himself was still a lay preacher. The Virginia Methodist preachers voted to break away from the Anglican Church, but Asbury, backed by Wesley, resisted. The end of the war and the independence of the American colonies changed the situation. Wesley sent over, by the hand of Dr. Coke, a letter which has become a famous document. Part of it has been quoted in another connection. In conclusion Wesley wrote:

> As our American brethren are now totally disentangled from the state and from the English hierarchy, we dare not entangle them again either with the one or the other. They are now at full liberty simply to follow the Scriptures and the primitive church. And we judge it best that they should stand fast in that liberty with which God has so strangely made them free.

(It seemed strange to Wesley that God should wish the American colonies to be free from Great Britain, an outcome to which he himself had been bitterly opposed.)

Wesley's letter was read to a conference which met on Christmas Eve, 1784, at Baltimore. The conference declared the independence of Methodism, adopted the name "The Methodist Episcopal Church," and ordained Asbury as deacon, elder, and superintendent. James O'Kelly and twelve others were ordained as elders. Simultaneously with counseling the American brethren to follow the primitive church and stand fast in their liberty, Wesley had appointed Asbury and Coke to be "superintendents" of American Methodism. Coke soon returned to England, and Asbury changed his own title to that of "bishop" and assumed such powers as no Anglican bishop or Methodist superintendent in England ever had. For one thing, Asbury assigned every preacher to his field, every presiding elder to his district, and from his assignments there was no appeal.

James O'Kelly had become a Methodist lay preacher in 1775, when he was about forty years old. He had been one of "Asbury's Ironsides," and had been the leader of those who urged an earlier separation from the Anglican Church. He had also led the futile protest against Asbury's assumption of the title of "bishop." Asbury had made him a presiding elder, but he continued to be the head and front of the resistance to the bishop's autocracy. When a demand for the "right of appeal" was voted down by a general conference in 1792, O'Kelly and a number of other preachers withdrew. A year later they organized the "Republican Methodist Church," with about thirty ministers and 1,000 members. This stage of the independent movement lasted only seven months.

On August 4, 1794, the Republican Methodists met in conference at Old Lebanon Church, in Surry County, Virginia, and adopted as their name "The Christian Church." This name was suggested by Rice Haggard, formerly a Methodist lay preacher and one of O'Kelly's partners in protest from the beginning. The members of the conference resolved, further, to take the Bible as their only creed. They had discovered, as one of them put it, that "the primitive church government, which came down from heaven, was a republic, though 'Christian Church' is its name." All preachers were to be on an equal footing. Ministers and laymen were to have liberty of private judgment. Conferences were to be merely advisory, and each congregation should "call its own pastor and enjoy the greatest possible freedom." It is to be noted that this secession from the Methodist Church involved no dissent from Methodist doctrine. It grew solely out of dissatisfaction with that church's system of government. The type of religious thought and preaching in the separated group remained substantially Methodist.

The new movement started with a staff of experienced and zealous ministers, under whose influence a considerable number of Methodist churches now became "Christian." The Methodist Church in Virginia and North Carolina suffered a net loss of 3,670, in spite of its vigorous evangelism, during the first year of the "Christian" church. Fifteen years later it was estimated that the Christian Church had 20,000 members "in the southern and western states." This doubtless includes Kentucky and Tennessee.

IN NEW ENGLAND, 1801

The first "Christian Church" in New England was about seven years later than the first in the South, and its origin was entirely unrelated to the earlier one. The New England movement got its impulse from the independent reactions of two young men against the type of religion they found in the Baptist churches of which they were members and in which they began to preach. These churches were Calvinistic in their emphasis on original sin, the limitation of the benefits of Christ's atonement to the "elect," the wrath of God toward sinners, the threat of hell, and the inability of man to do anything for his own salvation.

Elias Smith, born in 1769 at Lyme, Connecticut, spent his boyhood under very crude frontier conditions in a new settlement in Vermont, and had a violent experience of conversion when a log fell on him in the woods. He joined the Baptist church, and began to preach when he was about twenty-one. In spite of his almost complete lack of education, the Baptist ministers of Boston ordained him two years later. For almost a decade he was a somewhat irregular Baptist preacher, improving his education by diligent private study, becoming more and more dissatisfied with orthodox Calvinism, seeking a way out of his confusion by independent study of the New Testament, and moving toward the conviction that the churches should abandon their theological and ecclesiastical systems and restore the simple faith and practice of the primitive church.

Abner Jones, born in 1772 at Royalton, Massachusetts, had a Vermont boyhood not unlike Smith's in its combination of frontier hardship, lack of schools, and torturing religious experience. Having achieved conversion, he joined the Baptist church, taught school for a time, then studied and practiced medicine by the short-cut "Thompsonian" system; but he also preached as opportunity offered. Still in his early twenties, he "quit the fellowship of the Calvinist Baptists," as his biographer testifies, after hearing Elias Smith preach, though Smith was then still a Baptist. As the result of his own thinking, stirred by Smith's influence, Jones organized an independent church at Lyndon, Vermont, in the Autumn of 1801, to which he would give no name but "Christian." This, says the historian of the movement, was "the first Christian church in New England." During the next year Jones secured ordination by three Free Will Baptist preachers—not as a Baptist but "only as a Christian"—and organized "Christian" churches at Hanover and Piermont, New Hampshire. Up to this time, Smith had been the leader in thought but had hesitated to break his Baptist ties. Jones now persuaded him to abandon the Baptist name and joined him in organizing a "Christian" church at Portsmouth, New Hampshire. In 1804 Jones moved to Boston and formed a church there.

These two men, Smith and Jones, lived and worked for nearly forty years after that. Jones established churches at Salem, Massachusetts, where he lived for several years, and at many other towns in New England, never striking root very deeply in any place but winning many followers to the movement and a number of preachers to its advocacy. Smith's most important contribution was the founding of a religious paper, the *Herald of Gospel Liberty*, the first issue of which was published on September 1, 1808, at Portsmouth, New Hampshire. With some slight intermissions and under a variety of names, finally returning to the original one, this journal was published for 122 years and then merged with the *Congregationalist*.

Within twenty years after the founding of that first "Christian" church at Lyndon, Vermont, there were dozens of such churches in New England and others in adjacent parts of Canada and in New York and Pennsylvania, all deriving from this original impulse. These were, on principle, independent churches. No organization directed or controlled them and they had no cooperative activities. However, there was a sense of fellowship among them and they soon began to hold informal conferences. There is record of a meeting of "the elders of the Christian Churches in the New England states, assembled at Portsmouth,

New Hampshire, June 23, 1809," which authorized a fraternal reply to a letter from representatives of the Christian Churches in Virginia and North Carolina. The "general conference" held at Windham, Connecticut, in 1816, and the series of "United States conferences" beginning in 1820 were really, in spite of their comprehensive names, only conferences of the churches in the northeastern states. One of these, in 1827, voted that it was not proper for ministers to use the title "Reverend" and passed a resolution condemning the use of instrumental music in public worship. About thirty regional conferences, by states or parts of states, had been organized within this area before 1832.

IN KENTUCKY, 1804

Third in order of time, but first in importance in relation to the Disciples, among the three movements which together constituted the "Christian Church" was the one in which Stone emerged as the leading figure.

Barton W. Stone, born in 1772 at Port Tobacco, Maryland, was a member of one of the oldest American families. His great-great-great-grandfather was the first Protestant governor of Maryland, 1648-53. Barton Stone's father, a man of some property, died just before the outbreak of the Revolutionary War, and his mother moved with her large family to Pittsylvania County, Virginia, very close to the North Carolina line. With his share of the money from his father's estate, Barton spent three years in David Caldwell's academy at Greensboro, North Carolina, thirty miles southwest of his home. Here he "completed the classical course" in 1793. This school was hospitable to revivalism. Caldwell himself was a Princeton graduate and a Presbyterian minister of the "New Light" type—that is, of evangelistic temper and with an easy tolerance in theology. McGready, the Presbyterian evangelist who was later to set southern Kentucky afire, came to Greensboro and converted most of the students. Stone was stirred by the appeal but repelled by the theology. Meanwhile his mother, who had been an Anglican, had become a Methodist. William Hodge, a young "New Light" Presbyterian, who had been one of Caldwell's boys, came preaching the love rather than the wrath of God. Stone abandoned his purpose to study law and decided to be that kind of Presbyterian preacher. The presbytery to which he applied for license directed him to prepare a trial sermon on the Trinity. He struggled with the theme, and his sermon was accepted, but he always had trouble with the doctrine of the Trinity.

While waiting for his license to preach, he went to Georgia to visit his brother and while there he served for about a year, beginning in January, 1795, as "professor of languages" in Succoth Academy, a Methodist school at Washington, Georgia. The principal of this academy was Hope Hull, a Methodist preacher who had been closely associated with O'Kelly in his protest at the Methodist conference two years earlier but who had remained with the Methodist Church when O'Kelly and the other insurgents withdrew to form the Christian Church. Stone and Hull became very intimate friends, and Stone accompanied Hull on a journey to Charleston, South Carolina, to attend a Methodist conference. John Springer, an ardently evangelistic Presbyterian preacher of the "New Light" type, whose field was only a few miles from the academy and who had the most cordial relations with the Baptists and Methodists in his neighborhood, became another counselor and friend and exercised, says Ware, a "decisive influence" on Stone.

Returning to North Carolina, Stone received his license to preach from the hands of the venerable and liberal Henry Pattillo, who, in a published sermon on "Divisions among Christians," had recommended the name "Christians" as the one "first given to the disciples by divine appointment at Antioch," and who declared that men ought to be permitted to differ peaceably about the doctrines of religion.

To summarize the influences of Stone's early background and environment, these items may be listed:

1. The Great Awakening, which, under the preaching of men trained in William Tennent's Log College and of George Whitefield, beginning about 1740 but echoing through the middle and southern colonies for more than half a century after that in the work of Samuel Davies and many other evangelistic or "New Light" Presbyterians, had stressed the common elements of the gospel and put the divisive doctrines of the creeds into a subordinate place.

2. The Methodist movement, which did not cease to be a revival when it became a church and which challenged the Calvinism of the Presbyterian creed.

3. The "Christian" Church, which was having its first rapid growth in Virginia and North Carolina while Stone was in the first formative stage of his ministry in the same region.

4. The direct and personal influence of the men who have been mentioned in the preceding paragraphs: David Caldwell, James McGready, William Hodge, Hope Hull, John Springer, and Henry Pattillo.

After an experimental and not very successful missionary trip which took him through the eastern part of North Carolina and back through Virginia, and feeling that there was a better field on the frontier, Stone headed west, on horseback again. Within three months he had ridden to Knoxville and, at some peril from Indians, on to Nashville (population 346 by the next census); had associated for a time with Thomas Craighead, a Princeton-trained Presbyterian preacher of independent mind, famous for his zeal for a "rational and scriptural evangelism" and his scant respect for the authority of creed and presbytery; had itinerated and preached in the Cumberland district of Tennessee; and had then crossed Cumberland Gap into Kentucky, spent a little time at Danville and Lexington, and by October, 1796, was installed as regular supply pastor of two Presbyterian churches at Cane Ridge and Concord. Cane Ridge was seven miles east of Paris; Concord, ten miles northeast of Cane Ridge.

The next year a call to the settled pastorate of his churches made it necessary for Stone to seek ordination from the Transylvania Presbytery. This would require a declaration of his adherence to the Westminster Confession. Renewed study did not resolve his doubts about the Trinity. Before facing the presbytery, he privately stated his trouble to James Blythe, then probably the most influential Presbyterian in Kentucky and later one of the severest critics of Stone's views. In the public ceremony, Stone declared his acceptance of the Confession "as far as I see it consistent with the Word of God." Upon that guarded statement he was ordained.

CANE RIDGE MEETING

The Great Western Revival, with which the names of Stone and Cane Ridge are closely associated, resulted from transplanting to Tennessee and Kentucky the methods of evangelistic appeal which had been used by "New Light" Presbyterians, Methodists, and "Christians" in the Southern states east of the mountains. Under frontier conditions it developed some bizarre and sensational features which have drawn attention away from its real values. It began gradually with the preaching of four or five men—especially James McGready and the brothers William and

John McGee—who had come west about the time Stone came, and who itinerated in Tennessee, near and north of Nashville, and the adjacent part of Kentucky. For three or four years the revival spirit grew and spread until the countryside was in a fever of excitement. Fantastic manifestations began to appear among persons who experienced "conviction of sin," and even among those who came to scoff—jerking and barking, hysterical laughter, falling and lying rigid like dead men. These were taken for manifestations of the power of the Holy Spirit.

Stone, who was concerned about religious apathy in his own parishes, traveled the nearly two hundred miles from Cane Ridge to Logan County in southwestern Kentucky, in the early spring of 1801, to see the revival in progress under the preaching of McGready. He was impressed with the genuineness of the revival. The physical demonstrations seemed to be "the work of God," but inexplicable and not wholly desirable. Stone was, in a sense, the advance agent of the revival as it moved north and east through Kentucky. By late spring it had reached the Bluegrass. On the Sundays of May and June, there were great meetings at churches in the area around Lexington, with attendance at the last three running to 4,000, then 8,000, then 10,000, according to contemporary estimates.

The climax came in the Cane Ridge camp meeting, which lasted from Friday to Wednesday, August 7-12, 1801. The crowd was estimated at 20,000. Many Presbyterian, several Methodist, and a few Baptist ministers preached, often simultaneously at different stations through the woods. The excitement was intense. The fantastic "exercises" occurred in great profusion. This meeting was held at Stone's church, and he had much to do with bringing it about, but it was not in any sense his meeting. It does not appear that he was the most prominent among the preachers. Richard McNemar, for example, was more conspicuous, and so was McNemar's nine-year-old daughter, who became a child prophetess and poured forth a torrent of exhortation from a perch on his shoulder. Stone rejoiced in the awakened interest in religion and in the salvation of many sinners, but the records do not show that he gave encouragement to the spectacular "exercises."

Not all the Presbyterians approved of this violent revivalism. Three features especially offended them: the opportunity it gave to preachers lacking education; the wild and disorderly physical "exercises"; and the stress upon the idea that "Christ died for all," not for a limited number, the elect. The issue about education was especially acute in southern Kentucky and became one of the grounds for the "Cumberland secession" and the formation of the Cumberland Presbyterian Church. The "exercises" gradually ceased to be a prominent feature of revivalism, except in remote and retarded communities, and left no permanent mark on any major group. While they lasted they prepared the way for an invasion by the Shakers, who won some temporary following. The declaration that Christ died for all raised a real theological issue. This was what the Methodists were preaching. So also were the "General" Baptists, who were distinguished from the "Particular" Baptists by their belief in a general atonement. Both kinds of Baptists were numerous in Kentucky, and the "Generals" later became a fertile field for the Reformers. Within two or three years after Cane Ridge the main wave had passed, but the camp meeting remained as a popular pattern of religious and social life, though without the more extreme features which had made the "great revival" spectacular.

Richard McNemar, a Presbyterian minister, had not only been a prominent figure at the Cane Ridge meeting but had elsewhere cooperated with the Methodists, whose type of evangelistic appeal was congenial to him. Three months after the meeting a heresy charge against McNemar was presented to his presbytery. The process was delayed because so many of the "revival men" took his part that those who had filed the charge hesitated to bring it to a vote. After various procedures in the presbytery, all irregular and indecisive, and after another minister, John Thompson, had become involved in the case, the Synod of Kentucky, meeting at Lexington, September 6-13, 1803, formally censured the presbytery for letting these two men continue to preach while the charge of holding "Arminian tenets" (i.e., Methodist doctrines) was pending against them.

As the synod was preparing to put McNemar and Thompson on trial, they presented to the synod a document signed by themselves and three others, protesting against the trial and withdrawing from the synod's jurisdiction. The other three were Barton W. Stone, John Dunlavy, and Robert Marshall. After a futile effort to win them back, the synod placed the five under suspension.

The Springfield Presbytery

These five men had left the Synod of Kentucky, not the Presbyterian Church. Their first act was to organize the Springfield Presbytery, independent of the synod. (Their "Springfield" is now Springdale, ten miles north of Cincinnati.) Their second act was to issue a statement of their position. This is a pamphlet of about 100 pages, the full title of which is: *An Abstract of an Apology for Renouncing the Jurisdiction of the Synod of Kentucky, Being a Compendious View of the Gospel and a few Remarks on the Confession of Faith*, with the names of the five attached as authors. The important points in this statement are: (1) Christ died for all—as against a limited atonement for the elect only. (2) The gospel itself is the means of regeneration, and faith is the act by which any man, if he will, can lay hold on that means. (3) Faith is the natural man's belief of testimony—a rational, as against a mystical, conception of faith. Nothing is said explicitly about either Christian union or the restoration of primitive Christianity. (William Guirey, a Virginia Christian minister, later sent a copy of this *Apology* to the New England Christians as expressing the sentiments of the Virginia-North Carolina group, and said that the Kentucky five "united with us" when they left the Presbyterians.)

So far, this was an anti-Calvinist movement within the Presbyterian Church. Its leaders admitted that their position was not in agreement with the Westminster Confession, but claimed the right to differ from the Confession where they thought it differed from the Scriptures. The whole history of "New Light" Presbyterianism in Virginia and the states south of it from colonial days, as well as the recent revival in Kentucky, gave them ground for saying: "We are not the only Presbyterians who view the doctrine of the atonement different from the Confession."

But the Springfield Presbytery was only a transition stage. These five men might make their independent presbytery the nucleus of a new Presbyterian body, as the Seceders and others had done in Scotland long before, and as the Cumberland Presbyterians were to do a little later; or they might cease to be Presbyterians. They chose the latter course. On June 28, 1804, less than a year after its organization, the Springfield Presbytery met at Cane Ridge and decreed its own dissolution. The document in which it recorded this action is called "The Last Will and Testament of the Springfield Presbytery." By this instrument, the presbytery willed "that this body die, be dissolved and sink into union with the

Body of Christ at large," that every congregation should be independent in the choice and support of its minister and the discipline of its members, and that the Bible alone should be their guide and standard. Ministers are not to be called "Reverend," are to "obtain license from God to preach the simple Gospel," and are to be supported by free-will offerings "without a written call or subscription." And finally, the Synod of Kentucky is exhorted to examine every suspect and suspend every heretic, "that the oppressed may go free and taste the sweets of gospel liberty." (The full text of the "Last Will and Testament" was reprinted in the first issue of Elias Smith's *Herald of Gospel Liberty*, Portsmouth, N. H., Sept. 1, 1808.)

THE CHRISTIAN CHURCH

At this same meeting, June 28, 1804, it was agreed that the name "Christian" should be adopted, to the exclusion of all sectarian names. This was suggested by Rice Haggard, who had made the same suggestion to the O'Kelly group ten years earlier when the Republican Methodists were looking for a new name. Haggard had been active as a minister of the Christian Church in North Carolina and Virginia from 1794 until his removal to Kentucky about the time of the Cane Ridge meeting.

The "Christians" of Kentucky immediately became a group of churches as well as a group of preachers. Fervid evangelists as they were, the ministers immediately won to the movement several of the Presbyterian churches for which they had preached and organized some new ones. By the end of 1804 there were at least thirteen Christian churches in north-central Kentucky and about seven more in southwestern Ohio. Presbyterians called it the "New Light schism." The number of preachers was increased by the adherence of a few revival Presbyterians, by the coming of some Christians from the East, and by recognizing as preachers a good many men who had little or no formal education.

Shaker missionaries came to Kentucky in 1805, attracted by reports of the marvelous manifestations of the Spirit in the great revival. McNemar and Dunlavy soon joined them.

In the new Christian Church, no question was at first raised about baptism. Within a few years, Stone came to the belief that only the immersion of believers was scriptural baptism, and this view spread gradually through the group. Stone immersed many, including some preachers, before he was himself immersed. But it was not made a test of fellowship. Twenty years later Stone wrote:

> It was unanimously agreed that every brother and sister should act according to their faith; that we should not judge one another for being baptized or for not being baptized in this mode. The far greater part of the church submitted to be baptized by immersion, and now [1827] there is not one in 500 among us who has not been immersed. From the commencement we have avoided controversy on this subject. (*Christian Messenger*, Vol. I, p. 267, Oct., 1827.)

This trend toward immersion existed only in the West. In the East it became a divisive issue in 1809, and only a minority adopted it. Immersion never became the common practice with the New England Christians.

For some time there was no organization among the Christian churches. A "general meeting" of the ministers was held at Bethel, Kentucky, August 8, 1810, at which they "agreed to unite themselves formally." This suggested to some the need of a clearer definition of doctrines, especially those of the Trinity, Christ, and the atonement. After statements had been drafted and discussed at a later meeting, it was agreed by almost all that freedom of theological opinion was better than conformity to a standard. Marshall and Thompson, feeling that the creedless Christians were too loose in doctrine, returned to the Presbyterian Church. This left only Stone, of the original five who had seceded from the synod on account of the heresy charges against McNemar and Thompson. So it was by survival, rather than by pre-eminence at the beginning, that Stone came to be considered the founding father of the Christian Church in Kentucky. Later, especially after he began the publication of the *Christian Messenger* in 1826, his leadership is evident; and in guiding the greater part of the Christian Church in the West into the merger with the Disciples, his influence was probably decisive.

The growth of the western Christian Church was not confined to Kentucky. It took root immediately in Tennessee and in southern Ohio and Indiana. Traveling evangelists went also into the South. As the tide of migration moved to new frontiers, unordained elders, farmer-preachers, and sometimes regular ministers carried it to Illinois, Missouri, and Iowa. The position of Kentucky, as a breeding ground of pioneers who went out in steady streams to aid in laying the foundations of these states, made it a strategic point from which a new religious movement might make its influence felt throughout the Middle West.

Such was the emphasis upon the independence of local churches and of preachers, and so firm the determination to avoid anything like the Presbyterian or Methodist systems of centralized control, that organization was slow and weak. That meeting in 1810, at which it was agreed to "unite formally," did not in fact lead to any formal organization. District conferences were arranged. There was a Deer Creek (Ohio) Conference as early as 1808, and in the following years there were many such. But as late as 1826, Stone felt it necessary to defend the practice of holding even district conferences for worship, to exchange news of the churches, to arrange appointments so as to supply destitute churches, and (a tentative suggestion) "for ordination, if thought proper," but emphatically with no authority over local churches. In the same year the Wabash (Indiana) Conference agreed that it would be well "to have a general conference established in some convenient place in the western states," but this was not done. The Christian Church in the West had nothing corresponding to what is now called "cooperative work," and no agencies or structures through which such work could be carried on. The churches of the Northeast had their so-called United States Conference, but sometimes they had qualms about so much ecclesiasticism. The (New England) general conference of 1832 voted to dissolve forever, but revived the next year.

Though there was no inclusive organization, the three main divisions of the Christian Church had some acquaintance with one another's work and a sense of being parts of one enterprise. The *Herald of Gospel Liberty* circulated widely. Stone had an agent in New York for his *Christian Messenger*. When he reported, in 1828, that "the sect called Christians have, in little more than a quarter of a century, risen from nothing to 1,500 congregations with a membership of 150,000," his estimate—doubtless much too large in any case—evidently includes all three, and his reference to "more than a quarter of a century" shows that he was thinking of beginnings earlier than the dissolution of the Springfield Presbytery.

CHAPTER V
THE COMING OF THE CAMPBELLS

Thomas Campbell, an Argyle Scot by lineage, was born in North Ireland in 1763, took a full classical course in the University of Glasgow, and after that the full course in the theological seminary of the Anti-Burgher section of the Seceder branch of the Scottish Presbyterian Church. After preaching and teaching for several years, he became the settled pastor of a church at Ahorey, in County Armaugh, thirty miles south of Belfast, where he remained from 1798 until 1807. Meanwhile he had married the daughter of a French Huguenot family, and his son Alexander had been born in 1788. While ministering to the Ahorey church, he also conducted a private academy at the neighboring town of Rich Hill. Throughout his life, Thomas Campbell devoted more of his time to teaching than to preaching.

The Seceder Presbyterians had split from the established Church of Scotland in 1733 in protest against the arrangement by which the right of appointing ministers had been taken from the parishes and given to lay "patrons," or landlords, for whom the right to appoint the parson went with their ownership of land. No question of doctrine was involved in this secession. The Seceders were, if anything, stricter Calvinists than the Church of Scotland. Later, the Seceders divided into Burghers and Anti-Burghers, and each of these into New Lights and Old Lights, on fine points concerning the relations of the church to the state. These divisions were carried from Scotland to Ireland, though the issues were irrelevant to conditions there. Thomas Campbell was an Old Light, Anti-Burgher Seceder Presbyterian. But he early outgrew any interest in these divisive issues and sought ways of promoting unity at least among the Seceders.

Aside from the odious examples of disunion before his eyes, two other influences drew Thomas Campbell toward a wider fellowship. One was the Independent (Congregational) church at Rich Hill, a church of the Scotch Independent type, strongly affected by the ideas of Glas and Sandeman and the Haldane brothers. Here he met the celebrated English evangelist, Rowland Hill, who preached an ardent gospel that took little account of sectarian boundaries, and the eccentric John Walker of Dublin, who left the Episcopal Church and resigned a fellowship in Trinity College to lead an independent movement. Campbell was already familiar with the writings of Glas and Sandeman and with the work of the Haldanes. None of these was explicitly an advocate of union; but they all played down the doctrines and creeds which create divisions and the ecclesiastical institutions which perpetuate them; and all played up a warm evangelical faith voluntarily accepted and a return to the simple practices of the New Testament church.

The second influence which moved Mr. Campbell toward a nonsectarian view of religion was the writings of the philosopher, John Locke, especially his *Letters Concerning Toleration*. In these essays Locke had urged toleration, not only by the state toward dissenting groups, but also by the church toward varieties of theological opinion within itself. Sentences could be quoted from Locke which sound as though they came straight from the *Declaration and Address*. All this rested on a philosophy carefully worked out in his *Essay on the Human Understanding*. Thomas Campbell diligently studied these two books by John Locke and made them required reading for his son Alexander, who never ceased to give them his unbounded admiration.

SECEDING FROM THE SECEDERS

Partly because of ill health in his forties (he lived to the age of ninety-one), and partly to find a place of ampler opportunity for his seven children, Thomas Campbell migrated to America in 1807, as many of his Ulster neighbors had done before him. He landed at Philadelphia on May 13, fortunately found the Associate Synod of North America, which represented all the Seceders in America, in session in that city, presented his credentials and was received into the synod on May 16, and two days later was appointed to the Presbytery of Chartiers in southwestern Pennsylvania. The minutes of the presbytery show that he had preaching appointments at "Buffaloe" (now Bethany, W. Va.), Pittsburgh, and other points beginning July 1. So, in less than three months after preaching his farewell sermon in the Ahorey church in Ireland, Thomas Campbell was ministering to a circuit of communities on the American frontier.

But the connection so promptly made was not long peacefully maintained. At the October meeting of the presbytery, another minister filed charges against him for heretical teaching and disorderly procedure, and others testified unfavorably. After several confused and stormy sessions, the presbytery suspended Mr. Campbell. He appealed to the synod in Philadelphia at its meeting the next year. There were extended and complicated proceedings, culminating in a formal trial in which he was found guilty on several counts, and was sentenced to be "rebuked and admonished." At the same time the synod censured the presbytery for its irregular and unfair handling of the case. Evidently the synod did not think too badly of Mr. Campbell, for it gave him appointments with the Philadelphia churches for the summer and then sent him back to resume his preaching in the Presbytery of Chartiers. But the presbytery, smarting under the synod's censure and the reversal of its act of suspension, gave him a chilly reception. Specifically, it failed to give him any preaching appointments, and a rule of the church forbade a preacher to make his own. Tensions and animosities developed until, on September 13, 1808, Thomas Campbell orally—and the next day in writing—renounced the authority of both presbytery and synod. From that act, severing his connection with the Seceder Presbyterians, Thomas Campbell never receded. But the presbytery continued to summon him to appear and answer charges until, a year and a half later, it gave him up as hopeless and voted to depose him "from the holy ministry and from the sealing ordinances."

What were the reasons for this break? Richardson, in his *Memoirs of Alexander Campbell*, says that Thomas Campbell gave offense first by inviting Presbyterians other than Seceders to participate in the communion service. This does not appear among the written charges in the minutes of either the presbytery or the synod, but it may well be true. He is quoted as saying that the test of fitness to commune should be only a "general," not a "particular," acceptance of the Westminster Confession, and that he himself would gladly commune with other Christians, Lutherans, for example, if a church of his own order were not available. Moreover, he admitted advising Seceders to attend the preaching services of other churches if none of their own was at hand.

The heart of the difficulty was that he said that "the church has no divine warrant for holding Confessions of Faith as terms of communion"; creeds may be useful for teaching, but they should not be used as tests of fellowship, because they contain some things that cannot be proved by the Bible and many things that ordinary people cannot understand. The only strictly theological point related to the nature of "saving faith," which, in Mr. Campbell's view, did not necessarily include a sense of "assurance that we in particular shall be saved." He had already moved far toward the conception of faith as the rational belief of testimony about Christ and trust in him, rather than a mystical experience evidencing a special act of divine grace in favor of the individual to assure him that he had been accepted by God. Two other complaints show that Mr. Campbell had been restless under the restraints of the Presbyterian system. He had preached, on invitation from the people, within the parish or circuit of another minister without getting his consent. And he had said that, in the absence of a minister, "ruling elders" (who would be laymen) might properly pray and exhort in public worship.

At this stage, then, it appears from the record that Thomas Campbell did not radically reject either the Calvinistic theology as a system of doctrine or the Presbyterian polity as a system of church government, though he was far on the way toward rejecting both. His divergence from the Seceder Presbyterians can be summed up under these points: (1) He wanted closer relations with Christians of other denominations. (2) He did not regard the creed as the standard of truth or as an authoritative compendium of the truths revealed in Scripture, but claimed for himself and for every Christian the right to be judged and to test the creed by reference to the plain teachings of the Bible. (3) He held that acceptance of the creed in detail should not be a condition of communion or fellowship. (4) He was suspicious of clerical monopoly. (5) He said that a feeling of assurance of salvation was not of the essence of saving faith, though it might accompany a high degree of such faith. (6) He held that Christ died for all men, and that any man could believe on him and be saved. This last point was his most definite departure from Calvinism.

If the presbytery gave Campbell no preaching appointments after the synod had sent him back "rebuked and admonished," naturally it gave him none after he had renounced its authority. But he continued to preach in private houses as opportunity offered. None of the churches for which he had preached followed him, and no Presbyterian ministers joined him in withdrawing from the Presbytery of Chartiers. In those respects his movement differed in its beginning from that of O'Kelly and from that of McNemar and Stone. But in both of the earlier secessions the separatists had been preaching in their districts for years, and the ground had been plowed by revivals, and in Kentucky the way had been prepared by the immigration of many "Christian" ministers and laymen from the East. Thomas Campbell, on the other hand, was a newcomer from Ireland and made the break in a community where there had been no such preparation and where he had no wide acquaintance.

Before the final action expelling Mr. Campbell from the Seceder Presbyterian ministry, a group of his sympathizers and habitual hearers, meeting at the home of Abraham Altars, between Mount Pleasant and Washington, Pennsylvania, resolved to form a society "to give more definiteness to the movement in which they had thus far been cooperating without any formal organization or definite arrangement." The result was the "Christian Association of Washington," organized August 17, 1809. It was agreed that a proper motto would be, "Where the Scriptures speak, we speak; where the Scriptures are silent, we are silent." One member protested that this would lead to giving up infant baptism. The others thought not, but considered it a sound principle wherever it might lead. To express more fully the motives and purposes of the association, Thomas Campbell drew up a *Declaration and Address*, which was presented at a subsequent meeting as the report of a committee of twenty-one. (The total membership was not much more.) On September 7, 1809, the association approved it and ordered it printed.

It was exactly at this point that Alexander Campbell arrived from Ireland by way of Scotland.

ALEXANDER CAMPBELL AT GLASGOW

When Thomas Campbell came to America, he left his family in Ireland. Alexander, then nineteen years old, was to conduct his father's school at Rich Hill until the end of the term and to bring his mother and the six younger children to America when his father gave the word. The word came when Thomas Campbell had been in America about fifteen months. On October 1, 1808, the family embarked at Londonderry. Their ship ran aground on one of the rocky islands of the Hebrides. During that experience, Alexander's previous thought about devoting himself to the ministry reached the point of a firm decision. The interruption of the voyage so late in the sailing season made it necessary to wait until spring for its continuance. The shipwrecked travelers made their way to Glasgow, where they remained almost an entire year.

This year in Glasgow proved to be very important. It gave Alexander opportunity to supplement the excellent instruction he had received from his father by a year of study in the University of Glasgow. In addition, it brought him into contact with the men from whom, as his biographer, Richardson, says, he derived "his first impulse as a religious reformer." These were representatives of the movement led and financed by the brothers Robert and James Alexander Haldane.

Alexander Campbell came to Glasgow with a letter of introduction to Mr. Greville Ewing, who was in charge of the seminary, or training school for lay preachers, which the Haldanes had established in that city. Mr. Ewing became his closest and most helpful friend during that year in Glasgow. Ewing had introduced into his seminary the books of Glas and Sandeman, whose teachings gave the strongest possible emphasis to the restoration of primitive Christianity in all details. In Ewing's conversation and Glas's and Sandeman's books, Alexander Campbell found not only the general concept of a needed restoration of primitive Christianity but such specific ideas as these: the independence of the local congregation; weekly observance of the Lord's Supper; a plurality of elders; the denial of clerical privileges and dignities; the right and duty of laymen to have a part in the edification and discipline of the church; and a conception of faith as such a belief of testimony as any man is capable of by the application of his natural intelligence to the facts supplied by Scripture. The Haldanes themselves, and some of the followers of Sandeman, had adopted immersion, but Ewing adhered to infant baptism and sprinkling.

The action of all these influences upon Alexander Campbell's mind, and of his mind upon what he saw and learned of Presbyterianism in Scotland, brought him to a profound dissatisfaction with it. He had no quarrel with its theology. Near the end of his year in Glasgow, when he was examined by the Seceder church to determine his fitness to partake of the communion—because he brought no credentials, and the Seceders were very careful to permit no unqualified person to commune—no fault was found with his profession of faith, and he received the "token" which would admit him to the table. But at the communion service, after postponing his decision to the last possible moment, he laid down his token and walked out. This was, in effect, his break with the Seceder Presbyterian Church. He never went back.

Alexander Campbell and the family sailed for America early in August, 1809, landed at New York on September 29, and proceeded to Philadelphia by stage-coach and thence westward by wagon. Word had been sent ahead to Thomas Campbell, and he met them on the road in western Pennsylvania, October 19, with a copy of the freshly printed *Declaration and Address* in his pocket. Father and son, with an ocean between them, had independently broken with their religious past and moved by converging paths toward the same goal. Alexander read the *Declaration and Address* and was enthusiastic about it. It marshaled him the way that he was going.

THE "DECLARATION AND ADDRESS"

The *Declaration and Address* is one of the most important documents in the history of the Disciples. It deserves not only reading in full but careful study. As published in a later edition, it is a pamphlet of fifty-six pages containing four parts: first, a Declaration (3 pages) stating briefly the plans and purposes of the Christian Association of Washington; second, an Address (18 pages), signed by Thomas Campbell and Thomas Acheson, giving an extended argument for the unity of all Christians and amplifying the principles on which the church can regain its original unity and purity; third, an Appendix (31 pages) explaining several points in the Address; fourth, a Postscript (3 pages), written three months later, suggesting steps to be taken for the promotion of the movement.

The Declaration states the aim and the means of attaining it. The aim: "unity, peace, and purity." The means: "rejecting human opinions, ... returning to, and holding fast by, the original standard." The method of procedure is outlined under nine heads:

> 1. The formation of a religious association "for the sole purpose of promoting simple evangelical Christianity, free from all mixture of human opinions and inventions of men."
>
> 2. Contributions "to support a pure Gospel Ministry, that shall reduce to practice that whole form of doctrine, worship, discipline, and government, expressly revealed and enjoined in the word of God."
>
> 3. The formation of similar societies.
>
> 4. The Christian Association of Washington is not a church, but an organization of "voluntary advocates for church reformation."
>
> 5. The association will support only such ministers as conform to "the original standard."

6. A committee of twenty-one, chosen annually, shall transact the business of the association.

7. Meetings shall be held twice a year.

8. An order of business for the meetings.

9. The association agrees to support those ministers whom it shall invite to assist "in promoting a pure evangelical reformation, by the simple preaching of the everlasting gospel, and the administration of its ordinances in an exact conformity to the Divine Standard."

The Address opens, and for many pages continues, with a picture of the "awful and distressing effects" of division among Christians, an impassioned plea for unity, an argument that conditions in America are uniquely favorable for a union effort, and a restatement of the causes of division and the basis of union. Mr. Campbell revealed the central principle of his endeavor, the ground of his hope for its success, and the breadth of his tolerance, when he wrote:

> It is, to us, a pleasing consideration that all the churches of Christ, which mutually acknowledge each other as such, are not only agreed in the great doctrines of faith and holiness; but are also materially agreed, as to the positive ordinances of Gospel institution; so that our differences, at most, are about the things in which the kingdom of God does not consist, that is, about matters of private opinion, or human invention.

The Address then lays down thirteen numbered propositions, which, in condensed form, are as follows:

1. "The church of Christ upon earth is essentially, intentionally, and constitutionally one."

2. Congregations locally separate ought to be in fellowship with one another.

3. Nothing ought to be an article of faith, a term of communion, or a rule for the constitution and management of the church except what is expressly taught by Christ and his apostles.

4. "The New Testament is as perfect a constitution for the worship, discipline and government of the New Testament church, and as perfect a rule for the particular duties of its

members; as the Old Testament was ... for ... the Old Testament Church."

5. The church can give no new commandments where the Scriptures are silent.

6. Inferences and deductions from Scripture may be true doctrine, but they are not binding on the consciences of Christians further than they perceive them to be so.

7. Creeds may be useful for instruction but must not be used as tests of fitness for membership in the church.

8. Full knowledge of all revealed truth is not necessary to entitle persons to membership, "neither should they, for this purpose, be required to make a profession more extensive than their knowledge." Realization of their need of salvation, faith in Christ as Savior, and obedience to him are all that is necessary.

9. All who are thus qualified should love each other as brothers and be united.

10. "Division among christians is a horrid evil."

11. Divisions have been caused, in some cases, by neglect of the expressly revealed will of God; in others, by assuming authority to make human opinions the test of fellowship or to introduce human inventions into the faith and practice of the church.

12. All that is needed for the purity and perfection of the church is that it receive those, and only those, who profess faith in Christ and obey him according to the Scriptures, that it retain them only so long as their conduct is in accord with their profession, that ministers teach only what is expressly revealed, and that all divine ordinances be observed as the New Testament church observed them.

13. When the church adopts necessary "expedients," they should be recognized for what they are and should not be confused with divine commands, so that they will give no occasion for division.

The Appendix explains and clarifies several points in the foregoing and answers possible objections.

The Postscript, written after the committee of twenty-one had held its first monthly meeting, December 14, 1809, makes two suggestions. The first is that there be prepared "a catechetical exhibition of the fulness and precision of the holy scriptures upon the entire subject of christianity—an exhibition of that complete system of faith and duty expressly contained in the sacred oracles; respecting the doctrine, worship, discipline, and government of the christian church." Fortunately, this was never done. The second suggestion is that a monthly magazine be published, to be called the *Christian Monitor*, to be started when 500 subscribers were secured, and to be devoted to "detecting and exposing the various anti-christian enormities, innovations and corruptions, which infect the christian church." This project also was dropped, and it was not until thirteen years later, and in the hands of Alexander Campbell, that the *Christian Baptist* took the assignment of "detecting and exposing."

At this distance in time it is not easy to see how the author and signers of the *Declaration and Address* could suppose that they would be able to "reduce to practice that whole form of doctrine, worship, discipline, and government, expressly revealed" without employing any opinions of their own in interpreting the revelation, when they clearly saw that those who had attempted this before them had produced discordant and divisive systems. They were sounding their prophetic and unifying note when they declared, in the same document, that the basis of fellowship is not agreement on any complete system of doctrine and church practice, but is the simple and saving essentials of the gospel upon which Christians generally are already agreed.

THE BRUSH RUN CHURCH

Alexander Campbell, newly arrived on the scene of this nascent reformation, immediately settled down to a strenuous course of private study—Bible, Greek, Hebrew, Latin, and church history. He preached his first sermon on July 15, 1810, in a private house. He had no license to preach and he was a member of no church, for he had left his Presbyterianism in Scotland, and the Christian Association of Washington was not yet a church. He preached a hundred times during the next twelve months.

After Thomas Campbell had applied for admission to the regular (not Seceder) Presbyterian Synod of Pittsburgh, and had been rejected, the Christian Association of Washington constituted itself a church, on May 4, 1811. This became the first church among Disciples of Christ in the Campbell strain of their lineage. The new church chose Thomas Campbell as elder, elected four deacons, and licensed Alexander Campbell to preach. It observed the Lord's Supper the next day, and thereafter every Lord's day. A simple building was erected—the Brush Run Church—and the first service was held in it on June 16, 1811. Alexander Campbell was ordained on the first day of the next January.

The subject of baptism had not yet been seriously considered. Some members of the group, and some of its critics, doubted whether the principles of the *Declaration and Address* were consistent with infant baptism and sprinkling. Thomas Campbell was not disturbed about it. Stating his views to the Synod of Pittsburgh, he had said that infant baptism is not a command of Christ, hence not a condition of membership in the church, but that it is a matter of forbearance. Three members of the Brush Run Church, soon after its organization, refused to commune because they had not been baptized. These had not even been sprinkled, yet they had been admitted to membership. "Forbearance" had extended so far. At their urgent request, Thomas Campbell immersed them—somewhat reluctantly, it may be surmised, for he did it without going into the water himself. At that time Alexander Campbell said: "As I am sure it is unscriptural to make this matter [baptism] a term of communion, I let it slip. I wish to think and let think on these matters."

Almost a year later, the birth of his first child forced the question of infant baptism upon his attention and drove him to a study of the whole subject. The result was the conviction that the sprinkling of infants was not baptism within the meaning of the New Testament. On June 12, 1812, Thomas and Alexander Campbell, their wives, and three other members of the church were immersed in Buffalo Creek by a Baptist preacher, on a simple confession of faith in Christ. Most of the members of the Brush Run Church soon followed this example. Those who did not, withdrew.

The adoption of immersion in this way, as the unvarying practice of the church and therefore as an item in the proposed platform for the union of all churches, radically changed the program of the movement. It had begun with the idea that the churches were divided by human opinions that had been added to a perfectly adequate common core of revealed truth and duty which all accepted. But now the Reformers could no longer say, as Thomas Campbell had said, that all the churches "are agreed in the great doctrines of faith and holiness and as to the positive ordinances of the Gospel institution." To achieve union no longer required only persuading the churches to unite upon something that they already held. Now, it became necessary to persuade them also to accept one "positive ordinance" which only the Baptists believed to be commanded in the New Testament.

But if the adoption of immersion erected a barrier between the Reformers and the other churches, it brought them closer to the Baptists. In the autumn of 1813 the Brush Run Church applied for admission to the Redstone Baptist Association, at the same time submitting a full written statement of its position, including its protest against creeds. The application was accepted, over the protest of some of the Baptist ministers. For the next seventeen years, the Reformers were, as Walter Scott said, "in the bosom of the Regular Baptist churches." But they did not lose their sense of mission or merge indistinguishably in the Baptist denomination.

CHAPTER VI
WITH THE BAPTISTS, 1813-30

After the Brush Run Church had joined the Redstone Baptist Association, Alexander Campbell began to preach more widely among the Baptist churches of the region. Thomas Campbell, who was more occupied with teaching than with preaching, rather rapidly dropped out of his position of leadership, which was taken over by his son. Alexander had married the daughter of a well-to-do farmer, and his father-in-law had deeded to him the farm which was to be the nucleus of his large Bethany estate, part of which became the campus of Bethany College thirty years later. Even at the age of twenty-five he enjoyed economic security and was well on the way toward becoming a substantial citizen.

At a meeting of the Redstone Baptist Association in August, 1816, Alexander Campbell preached his famous "Sermon on the Law." There seems to have been some scheming to keep him off the program, and he was called in only at the last moment to fill a vacancy. But the content of the sermon, if not its form, had evidently been the subject of long and careful study. The central point of it was that the Christian system is not a continuation of the Jewish regime but is based on a new covenant which, though prepared for and prophesied in the religion of the Old Testament, is a radically new thing. Therefore, he said, no arguments can be drawn from the Old Testament about the nature or form of Christian institutions. The law of the Sabbath has nothing to do with the observance of the first day of the week; baptism cannot be understood by considering it as taking the place of circumcision; paying tithes and keeping fasts are no part of a Christian's duty; and any alliance between church and state, as in the old covenant of God with the Hebrews, is alien to the spirit and nature of Christianity.

Some of these conclusions—especially separation of church and state and the denial of any analogy between baptism and circumcision—were pleasing to the Baptist audience. But the basis of the argument, the complete abrogation of the Old Testament law, seemed to many a dangerous doctrine. The preachers who heard the sermon went out to spread among the churches their fears that this bold and brilliant young man might be a disturber of Baptist usage. Thereafter he "itinerated less" among the Baptist churches and confined his labors to "three or four little communities constituted on the Bible, one in Ohio, one in Virginia and two in Pennsylvania." But he also made one or two preaching trips a year among the regular Baptists. He opened in 1818, and conducted for four years, a boarding school for boys, especially with a view to finding and training candidates for the ministry.

DEBATES ON BAPTISM

Mr. Campbell's Baptist colleagues may have considered him heretical about the covenants, but they could not fail to value him as a champion of immersion. So when a Seceder Presbyterian minister, John Walker of Mt. Pleasant, Ohio, issued a challenge for a debate on that topic, they urged him to accept it. Mr. Walker, as challenger, affirmed that the infant children of believers are proper subjects for baptism and that sprinkling is a proper mode. As to the baptism of infants, he rested his case almost wholly on the proposition "that baptism came in the room of circumcision, that the covenant on which the Jewish church was built and to which circumcision is the seal, is the same with the covenant on which the Christian church is built and to which Baptism is the seal." This is precisely the proposition that Mr. Campbell had denied in his "Sermon on the Law," and it gave him opportunity to elaborate and reinforce his argument as to the radical newness of Christianity and its freedom from Old Testament law. In addition, he made use of his careful studies of the Greek word *baptizein* and the prepositions used with it in the passages describing baptism. He quoted pedobaptist lexicographers and commentators to prove that the Greek verb means "to immerse"; and he stressed the distinction between "positive" and "moral" precepts to show that the former, including baptism, demand implicit obedience with no reasoning on our part as to the expediency or value of the thing commanded.

The debate with Walker was held at Mt. Pleasant, Ohio, in June, 1820. It greatly enhanced Campbell's reputation, especially among the Baptists of the Mahoning Association in eastern Ohio, and brought him many invitations to preach in the churches of this association. The publication of the debate as a book gave much wider publicity to his ideas and brought on another debate, in October, 1823, with W. L. Maccalla, a Presbyterian minister of Augusta, Kentucky. This debate was held at Washington, Mason County, Kentucky. On the horseback trip from his home to that place, Mr. Campbell was accompanied by Sidney Rigdon, then a young Baptist minister in Pittsburgh, later one of the three who constituted the "first presidency" of the Mormon Church and still later a rival of Brigham Young for its leadership after the death of the "prophet" Joseph Smith. The text of Campbell's side of the discussion, as subsequently published, is based on Rigdon's report.

In the Maccalla debate, Campbell began to develop his theory of the design of baptism. Baptism is appropriate for penitent believers, not for innocent infants, because it is the "washing of regeneration," designed to cleanse, not from inherited original sin, but from the guilt of actual personal sins. Yet it is not a magical "water salvation," though he was often accused of teaching that. "The blood of Christ *really* cleanses us who believe.... The water of baptism *formally* washes away our sins." This distinction was never again so clearly stated, and it may be argued that it represents a stage through which Mr. Campbell's thought passed, rather than a conclusion on which it rested. However, it brought into prominence the conception of "baptism for the remission of sins." When the distinction between "real" and "formal" remission was dropped, other ways were found for avoiding the morally repugnant conclusion that, if remission comes by baptism and only immersion is baptism, then the unimmersed must necessarily be damned. Neither Campbell nor the Disciples after him ever believed that.

The journey to Kentucky to meet Maccalla was the first of Alexander Campbell's many visits to Kentucky. It put him in touch with men and churches that were going his way—the "Christians," and a strain among the Baptists that was to furnish powerful reinforcement to his cause. And on that long journey by horseback he carried in his saddlebags copies of the first issue of his new magazine, the *Christian Baptist*.

"REFORMING BAPTISTS"

The *Christian Baptist* began in 1823 and continued for seven years. Mr. Campbell was his own publisher. He set up a printing office on his farm, secured the location of the post office of Buffaloe (later Bethany), and was appointed postmaster. The magazine took up at once the delayed task of "detecting and exposing the various anti-christian enormities, innovations and corruptions which infect the christian church." It was small, as a hornet is small, and its sting was as keen. It attacked especially three characteristics of the existing churches: the authority and status assumed by the clergy; unscriptural organizations, such as synods and church courts, missionary societies, Bible societies, Sunday considerable following from the previously unconverted as well as from the Baptist churches. By the end of 1830, the Reformers—"Campbellites" to their opponents—were a clearly recognizable element in Kentucky, though most of them were still nominally Baptists.

WALTER SCOTT, THE "GOSPEL RESTORED"

But the events which were most decisive in changing the Reformers from "Reforming Baptists" to an independent group to be known as Disciples occurred in the Mahoning Association in eastern Ohio. The man who had most to do with these events was Walter Scott. Born in Edinburgh in 1796 and educated in the university of that city, Scott was still a member of the Church of Scotland when he came to New York immediately after his graduation and to Pittsburgh the next year. Here he taught in a school conducted by a Mr. Forrester, who was also the leader of a church of immersed Haldaneans—locally known as "kissing Baptists." Scott joined this church. To gain a better understanding of the restoration of primitive practices, he visited similar churches in New York, Paterson, New Jersey, Baltimore, and Washington. He found that they did not entirely agree as to just what the practice of the primitive church was. He returned to Pittsburgh much depressed, but resumed his teaching and studied the writings of Locke, Glas, Sandeman, and Haldane to clarify his religious ideas. The sudden death of Mr. Forrester threw upon him the care of the little church. His first meeting with Mr. Campbell, his senior by eight years, was at Pittsburgh in the winter of 1821-22. They met occasionally during the next year, and the contact brought Scott out of his fog. When Campbell was planning his magazine, it was Scott who suggested the name, "Christian Baptist," as an indication that the aim was to work with and through the Baptists, not to promote a defection from them.

Scott's chief interest was in defining the process by which one becomes a Christian. That had really been the central point in Thomas Campbell's original concern, for this, in his view, would define the terms of fellowship and become the basis of union. But attention had been diverted to developing a complete pattern for the restoration of the church on the primitive model. To the first four issues of the *Christian Baptist*, Scott contributed a series of articles on "A Divinely Authorized Plan of Preaching the Christian Religion." The plan of preaching it and the plan of accepting it must naturally be the same. There must be the right elements in the right order. He found that the exact steps, authoritatively given as constituting the way to salvation, were these: (1) Faith, the persuasion of the mind by rational evidence. "The messiahship rests on demonstration," and everything else follows from that on authority. (2) Repentance of sins, under the motive of the promises. (3) Baptism, in obedience to divine command. (4) Remission of sins, and (5) the gift of the Holy Spirit, both in fulfillment of God's promise, which is conditioned on man's completion of the first three steps.

These became the five points of Scott's standard sermon and the outline of a tremendously effective evangelistic appeal. These points were all implicit in what Campbell was teaching, but so long as they remained implicit they could not win converts; they could only change some regular Baptists into Reforming Baptists, and divide Baptist churches and associations. The Mahoning Association was more thoroughly imbued with Campbell's views than any other; yet at its annual meeting in 1827 all its churches together (excepting Campbell's own church at Wellsburg, which did a little better) reported only twenty-one additions for the year—and there had been twelve excommunications. It was agreed to appoint an evangelist to "travel and teach among the churches." Scott, who had moved to Steubenville, Ohio, within the boundaries of the association, and who had visited its meetings twice at Campbell's invitation and preached before it once, was asked to accept this appointment. He was not a member of the association, not a Baptist, not an ordained minister. With the Mahoning Association in 1827, evidently being a Reformer counted for more than being a Baptist.

It was a good appointment. Scott began his work at New Lisbon, Ohio. The first convert under his new presentation of the "ancient gospel" was William Amend, who, according to Scott's biographer, Baxter, "was beyond all question the first person in modern times who received the ordinance of baptism in perfect accordance with apostolic teaching and usage." That was on November 18, 1827. The force and freshness of Scott's appeal, the exciting sense of discovery, the thought that an ancient treasure of divine truth was just now being brought to light after being lost for centuries, the sense of witnessing the dawn of a new epoch in the history of Christianity—these things gave to the campaign an extraordinary quality. It was different from other revivals. Here was no debauch of emotion, but an attractive blending of rationality and authority. It appealed to common sense as well as to Scripture. It assumed man's rational ability to understand what he ought to do and why, and his moral ability to do it. The first three steps were man's; the other two were God's. When the convert had believed, repented, and obeyed (i.e., been baptized), he could be perfectly sure that he would be saved by the remission of his sins and the gift of the Holy Spirit and eternal life. He had the promise of God for it.

Scott's work extended throughout eastern Ohio. Besides completing the conquest of the Mahoning Association for the Reform, it gained great numbers of converts—many from other denominations but many also, probably more, who had been members of no church. New churches were organized. Some of the Baptist preachers entered vigorously into the new movement, and some of the new converts—such as William Hayden, A. S. Hayden, and John Henry—became preachers of great power. The first year of this new evangelism brought more than 1,000 additions to the churches of the Mahoning Association, more than doubling their total membership. Scott was assisted at times by Joseph Gaston, a "Christian" preacher who was, Scott says, the first of that church who "received the gospel after its restoration." At the 1828 meeting of the association, William Hayden was added to the staff, and the next year Bentley and Bosworth.

SEPARATION FROM THE BAPTISTS

In three years, the Mahoning Association had lost every distinctive Baptist characteristic except its form and name as a Baptist association. Scott's rigid devotion to the idea of reproducing the practice of the primitive church led him to the conviction that there was no warrant for associations. He suggested that the association be dissolved and persuaded Mr. Campbell not to oppose this action, as he was inclined to do. A resolution to that effect was passed.

The actual separation of the Reformers—hereafter to be called Disciples—from the Baptists was a process which had begun two or three years earlier and which continued for at least three years after this event. But if a single date must be set for the beginning of the Disciples of Christ as a separate and independent religious body, it is in August, 1830, with the dissolution of the Mahoning Association at Austintown, Ohio.

The doctrines and practices of the Disciples which distinguished them from the Baptists at the time of the separation may be summarized:

As to doctrine: (1) The distinction between the old and new covenants, with consequent reliance solely upon the New Testament as a source for instruction concerning Christian faith and institutions. (2) The design of baptism, for remission of sins; faith, repentance, and baptism constitute regeneration. (3) The nature of faith as the belief of testimony, a rational act of which any man is capable in the exercise of his natural powers and free will. (4) The operation of the Holy Spirit through the Word alone in conversion. (5) Rejection of the Calvinistic idea (which not all Baptists held) that Christ died for only the "elect," a limited number of predetermined individuals.

As to practice: (1) Rejection of creeds and church covenants. (2) Reception of members on confession of faith in Christ, repentance, and baptism, without examination, the relation of an "experience," or a vote by the congregation. (3) Baptism and the Lord's Supper may be administered by any believer. (4) Weekly observance of the Lord's Supper. (5) No special "call" to the ministry expected or required and, in general, no sharp distinction between clergy and laity. (6) Denial of the authority of associations to exercise any power over local congregations (Baptists also denied this in theory), or to pass any judgment upon them, or to lay down conditions of fellowship and communion, as Baptist associations did when they excluded delegates who did not bring assurance that their churches adhered to the Philadelphia Confession.

While the movement toward separation from the Baptists was approaching its crisis, two events occurred, both in 1829, which added greatly to the fame and prestige of Alexander Campbell and thus helped indirectly to get the Disciples off to a good start.

Mr. Campbell was elected and served as a member of the Virginia Constitutional Convention. He answered those who criticized this entry into politics by saying that he wanted to urge the abolition of slavery or at least some steps in that direction. But he found that it would be impossible to do anything about slavery until the system of representation was so altered as to take away the concentration of power that was in the hands of the slave-owning aristocracy in the eastern part of the state. He fought a magnificent but losing fight on the floor of the convention for the abolition of the property qualification for voting and for representation in proportion to population. In advocating these democratic measures he faced, almost alone, such champions as John Marshall, John Randolph, and ex-presidents Madison and

Monroe, all of whom were members of the convention. Anyone who doubts the intellectual and moral stature of Alexander Campbell will find a convincing demonstration of both by reading, in the published proceedings of the convention, his speeches in debate with these giants.

A few months earlier, Mr. Campbell had engaged in a debate with the noted British social reformer, philanthropist, and skeptic, Robert Owen, on the general subject of the validity of the claims of Christianity and a religious versus a secular and materialistic view of the world. In his two earlier debates he had represented the Baptists against the Presbyterians. In his two later ones, he defended Protestantism against Roman Catholicism and certain aspects of the Disciples' position against its critics. But in the debate with Owen he had his most eminent opponent and his most exalted theme—the "Evidences of Christianity." For this occasion he was not the advocate of a party or a particular system of religious ideas, but was the champion of all Christianity. His own movement entered upon its independent existence with some of the glory of this splendid performance upon it.

CHAPTER VII
FIRST YEARS OF INDEPENDENCE, 1830-49

With the dissolution of the Mahoning Association, the Disciples became a separate people with churches of their own, which were generally called "Churches of Christ." The disbanding of several Baptist associations in Kentucky within the next few months and the division of others added to the number of churches in the new body. Scattered through the entire area which had been affected by the teaching of Mr. Campbell and the *Christian Baptist* were many churches which were ready to follow the Reform, or had already begun to do so. Some of these voluntarily withdrew from the Baptist associations with which they were connected; others were put out. And in Baptist churches which adhered to their old position, the individuals or minority groups who accepted the new way were generally excluded. One point should be made clear: there is no known record of any case in which the Reforming, or Disciple, element in what had been a Baptist church ever excluded those who insisted on continuing to be Baptists.

By 1833 the Disciples had been pretty thoroughly eliminated from the Baptist churches, to the number of something like twenty thousand members, nearly all in Ohio, Pennsylvania, Virginia, Kentucky, and Tennessee. Their most important accomplishments during the next two decades were: the growth of a conscious fellowship and the sense of being a united group; the union with the greater part of the western "Christian" churches; the development of institutions, customs, and procedures by which their common life and purpose could be expressed; and a remarkable increase in numbers and geographical extent.

Mr. Campbell brought the *Christian Baptist* to an end with the completion of its seventh volume and immediately began the publication of the *Millennial Harbinger*, January, 1830. This was a larger magazine, devoted less to "detecting and exposing" the corruptions of the divided churches than to presenting a constructive program for curing their ills. Moreover, it had the responsibility, as the earlier magazine had not, of reporting the news of a movement which had now become a going concern and of discussing the problems which arose in the life of the new body. The name does not indicate any special interest in what is generally called the "millennium," as implying a visible second coming of Christ in the near future. The kind of millennium of which this magazine proposed to be the harbinger was the triumph of the Kingdom of God on earth. If that was ever to come, the editor thought, it could be only when the church had been purified and united.

The *Millennial Harbinger* appeared monthly from 1830 to 1870. Mr. Campbell was its editor for nearly thirty years. During this time it was the backbone of Disciples' periodical literature. A great many small monthlies very soon began to spring up. Most of them had small circulation and short life, but their total influence was great, and a few became important. A list printed in 1845, and not claiming to be complete, names fifteen monthlies and two weeklies in existence at that time.

DISCIPLES AND CHRISTIANS

The union between the Disciples and the Christian churches in Kentucky and adjacent states west of the Alleghenies was an event of the utmost importance for the whole movement. Since the churches of both groups exercised a high degree of local independence, union could not have been brought about by any binding act of conferences or conventions, even if there had been general conferences or conventions in either party, as there were not. It had to depend upon a contagion of fellowship between their congregations in many communities. But the process was rapid, and the union may be dated as of 1832. It began with a consultation among some of their leaders on the first day of that year and was far enough advanced to insure its success before the end of the year.

Barton W. Stone and Alexander Campbell first met in 1824. They were friends from the start, and both were impressed by the similarity of their pleas for simple and evangelical Christianity. In 1826 Mr. Stone began the publication of a monthly, the *Christian Messenger*, at Georgetown, Kentucky. In a communion having no general organization and no cooperative work, it was his position as editor which, more than anything else, gave him the prominence that has led to calling the Christian church in Kentucky, not very accurately, "the Stone movement." Since he wrote constantly and copiously for his magazine and also published reports of the activities of the churches and evangelists, it gives a good contemporary picture of his mind and of the principles and practices of the Christian churches during the years immediately before the union.

The unity of all Christians was the theme of a series of articles which began in the first issue of the *Christian Messenger*, and the topic frequently recurs. Stone gives the arguments for unity and states and answers the possible objections. The principal obstacle to union, as he sees it, is insistence upon doctrinal agreement. Stone is for tolerance on all matters of opinion. Yet there are some doctrines in the orthodox creeds which Stone considers so erroneous that he is not content to say that they ought not to be made tests of fellowship; he must try to disprove them and eliminate them from the minds of all Christians. These are the generally accepted doctrines of the Trinity, the nature of Christ, and the atonement. Upon each of these subjects Mr. Stone wrote many long articles and editorials. He did not hesitate to say that "we deny the Trinity," not because it is mysterious but because it is not a revealed doctrine. The character of God is revealed, but not his essence or the mode of his existence. Christ was the Son of God, being of the same nature but not of the same substance. The Holy Spirit "means the power or energy of God, never a third person in deity."

It is not surprising that the orthodox denominations regarded the writer of these statements as a dangerous man and the "Christians" as rank heretics. The orthodox, and especially the Presbyterians, would have been sensitive about such statements at any time; but just at this time they were in a more than usually suspicious mood, for the first year of the *Christian Messenger* (1826) was the very year in which the Unitarian, Dr. Horace Holley, had been dismissed from the presidency of Transylvania University, and Kentucky was still ringing with the conflict between the orthodox and the "liberals." So it was inevitable that the charge of "Unitarianism" should be hurled at Stone and his party. In the eyes of his most bitter critics, Stone was also a "Crypto-Arian" and a "Crypto-Socinian." Controversial pamphlets flew back and forth. As one reads them now, Stone seems to hold his own in theological scholarship and English style, and they cast no cloud upon his devotion to Christ or upon his zeal for the union of Christ's followers in one family of faith and the salvation of sinners by the power of the gospel. Stone was anti-Calvinist, anti-Trinitarian, anticreed, but he was *not* a Unitarian.

LIKENESSES AND DIFFERENCES

Studying Campbell's *Christian Baptist* and *Millennial Harbinger* and Stone's *Christian Messenger* for the period shortly before the union of the two movements, one finds the evidence of some important likenesses and of certain differences, which were soon adjusted without much trouble. The likenesses were these:

1. Both groups consciously and explicitly aimed to promote the union of Christians.

2. Both rejected creeds and theologies as tests of fellowship, insisted on liberty of opinion on all matters of doctrine that were not considered as unmistakably revealed, and held that simple faith in Christ was sufficient.

3. They agreed that Christ died for all and that all could believe on him and be saved.

4. They agreed that saving faith, at least in its minimum essentials, was nothing else than an act of the mind in accepting rational evidence of the truth, and that even fallen and sinful man was capable of that act without special assistance from the Holy Spirit. This idea was prominent in Campbell's thought, and it was fundamental in Scott's method, which gave the Reformers their evangelistic drive. Stone had expressed the same idea earlier but he did not make much use of it, and the evangelism of the Christians does not seem to have been greatly affected by it.

5. The practice of believers' baptism by immersion and the conception of baptism for the remission of sins were common to both, subject to some limitations to be mentioned presently.

6. Both opposed the use of unscriptural names as sectarian and divisive. On Stone's side there was much argument that Acts 11:26 ("The disciples were called Christians first in Antioch") meant that they were so called by divine appointment, so that this name *must* be used. But this extreme opinion was not insisted upon, and Campbell's preference for "Disciples" was no obstacle. The use of the two names—and of "Churches of Christ" as well—confused the public but was no barrier to union.

Replying to a correspondent who asked why the Christians should not unite with the "New Testament Baptists" (meaning Campbell's Reformers), Stone wrote in 1828: "If there is a difference between us, we know it not. We have nothing in us to prevent a union; and if they have nothing in them in opposition to it, we are in spirit one. May God strengthen the cords of Christian union."

But there were some differences of emphasis and practice. The chief differences were these:

1. The Christians did not make immersion a condition of membership. Most of them had been immersed, but they considered baptism as lying in the field of opinion, in which there should be liberty. Stone repeatedly defended this position. In 1830 he wrote: "These reforming Baptists are engaged in a good work. They proclaim union with all who believe the simple facts of revelation and manifest their faith by their works of holiness and love, without any regard to the opinions they may have formed of truth. Should they make their own peculiar views of immersion a term of fellowship, it will be impossible for them to repel successfully the imputation of being sectarians and of having an authoritative creed (though not written) of one article at least, which is formed of their own opinion of truth; and this short creed would exclude more Christians from union than any creed with which I am acquainted." Yet only a few months later he admitted feeling some inconsistency between preaching immersion for remission of sins and admitting to church membership without it. "When asked for our divine authority from the New Testament, we have none that can fully satisfy our own minds. In this state our minds have labored, and are still laboring." (*Christian Messenger*, Vol. IV, pp. 200, 275.)

2. The Christians had at least the beginnings of a method of obtaining a responsible ministry. Stone criticized those who thought that a church could "induct into the ministerial office"; that function belongs to the "bishops and elders." If a minister is charged with "preaching doctrine contrary to the gospel," he should be examined by a "conference of bishops and elders." The idea was that the ministry as a whole, or by conference groups, should have power to protect the churches against erratic or unworthy ministers. There is no evidence that such control was actually exercised, but even the idea of such control was alien to the Disciples until much later, and still is with most of them. But at the time of the union, the Christians seem to have had a somewhat "higher" conception of the office of the ministry.

3. The Christians were much more zealous in evangelism than the Reformers had been before the outburst of evangelistic fervor with John Smith and a few other "New Testament Baptists" in Kentucky and the campaign of Walter Scott in Ohio in 1827. But their method of evangelism had been of the Methodist type. There is clear evidence that theirs was, in practice, a "mourners' bench" revivalism, in spite of Stone's theory of faith as a rational act. Christian evangelists, sending to Stone's paper the reports of

their meetings, write that "crowds of mourners came forward weeping and crying for mercy"; or, "the preachers had a good measure of the Holy Ghost and ... several [hearers] appeared to be cut to the heart and were crying for mercy"; or, "crowds of weeping mourners came forward to unite with us in prayer"; or, more specifically, that the summer camp meetings (in Georgia) are "conducted in the main in the manner of Methodist camp meetings." Scott's new method of presenting the "Gospel restored" in clear steps created some surprise and questioning. A Christian preacher writes: "His method and manner are somewhat novel to me.... He seems to suppose the apostolical gospel to consist of the use of the following particulars: faith, repentance, baptism for remission of sins, the gift of the Holy Spirit, and eternal life. Thus, you see, he baptizes the subject previous to the remission of his sins or the receiving of the Holy Spirit." Stone replies: "We have for some time practiced in this way throughout our country." Evidently Stone had already come to a position identical with that of Campbell and Scott as to the nature of faith, the purpose of baptism, and the technique of evangelism. But just as evidently, the Christian preachers and churches generally had not. They had zeal for evangelism, but they still had much to learn about its method. Scott was their teacher.

4. Whereas the Reformers early adopted the practice of observing the Lord's Supper every Sunday, the Christians did not. By 1830, Stone had decided that this was the practice of the early church, and he wrote: "Whenever the church shall be restored to her former glory, she will again receive the Lord's Supper every first day of the week." But he was less ardent than Campbell about "restoring the ancient order of things," and he was disposed to be patient about this as he was about immersion.

UNION AND GROWTH

By 1830 the Christian churches west of the Alleghenies had, it is estimated, seven or eight thousand members in Kentucky, somewhat fewer in Tennessee, and smaller numbers in all the states to which migrants had been going from these two. There were district conferences in Ohio and Indiana, in Alabama and Mississippi; a Christian church organized in Missouri in 1816 was only the first of several; and there were two conferences in Iowa by 1828.

The growing acquaintance and sympathy between Christians and Disciples led to a number of consultations between their leaders at various places in Kentucky, and finally to a meeting at Lexington, January 1, 1832, attended by prominent representatives of both. It was unanimously agreed that they should unite. Since neither group recognized any church authority superior to the local congregation, actual union could be accomplished only by going to the congregations and persuading them to unite. "Raccoon" John Smith (Disciple) and John Rogers (Christian) went out as a team to carry this message to the churches. Others took it up. Stone's *Christian Messenger* and Campbell's *Millennial Harbinger* supported it. Within three years the greater part of the Christian churches in the area mentioned had joined the merger. On the points of difference, especially baptism and evangelistic method, the practice of Campbell and Scott prevailed. The Christians contributed a revived emphasis upon liberty of opinion and upon union, which the Reformers had been in danger of subordinating in their zeal for the restoration of "a particular ecclesiastical order."

There had been, up to this time, no organizational connection among the three great groups of "Christian" churches. Those in New England and those in the southern Atlantic states were not affected by the merger with the Disciples. They tightened their denominational organization and continued their separate existence until, nearly a hundred years later (1930), they united with the Congregationalists.

It is not possible to give a clear picture of the numerical growth and geographical expansion of the Disciples in their first twenty years. There were at first no organizations to promote the movement, no headquarters to project plans, no agencies to collect statistics, no yearbook to list churches and preachers. The energy of the movement was tremendous. As a plea for union, its appeal was to Christians of all faiths; therefore there was no hesitation about proselyting. As a presentation of the way of salvation, its message was to the unconverted. Both classes responded in large numbers. This "Gospel restored"—Scott's five steps in conversion—and the call to union on that basis were a simple message. One had only to hear it to believe it, and almost anyone who believed it could preach it—and a great many did. Most of those who evangelized went out on their own initiative and responsibility. The frontier was open, and there was a steady flow of migration to the west. Among the migrants were many preachers, who were often farmers also. But if there was no preacher in the new community, laymen might carry the message and plant the seed of a church. The distinction between ministers and laymen was often very vague. One who could preach became *ipso facto* a preacher. Besides farmer-preachers, there were lawyers, doctors, teachers, and merchants who preached, won converts, baptized them, and established churches.

The need of some simple and efficient method of cooperation was soon felt. Some doubted whether any organization of the churches was scriptural. But the decision of most was that organized cooperation among the churches to spread the gospel—but *not* to exercise authority over the churches—was a proper expedient. A meeting of representatives of several churches at New Lisbon, Ohio, in 1831, and another at Wheeling, West Virginia, in 1835, reached this conclusion and considered ways and means of cooperation. A few glimpses, almost at random, at the beginnings of churches and organizations in certain states will indicate something of the method and rate of expansion during these two decades.

In Indiana, several local movements, some beginning as early as 1810, contributed to the stream of the Reform. Some Free Will Baptists, regular Baptists, Dunkers, and "Christians" had arrived independently at similar ideas, and presently the *Christian Baptist* helped to unify them, and the merging of the Disciples and Christians completed the process. Their first cooperation for a specific purpose was when five churches joined in supporting John O'Kane as an evangelist, and his first work was to organize the First Church in Indianapolis in 1833. Indiana's first state convention was held in 1839, with fifty preachers present and reports of 115 churches with over 7,000 members. The state missionary society was formed ten years later. But the growth in numbers and churches—and it was rapid and substantial—was due to the work of individuals, local churches, and county cooperation more than to the state organization.

The first Disciples in Illinois came from Kentucky and Indiana in 1830. Stone visited Jacksonville in 1832, preparatory to moving there two years later. He found a Christian church and a Disciple church, and persuaded them to unite. In 1834 a group of churches in that vicinity voted to employ an evangelist and issued an invitation to a state meeting. But the first state meeting was not held until 1842.

To Missouri came the Christian preacher, Thomas McBride, from Kentucky in 1816, followed soon by Joel Haden, T. M. Allen, and others. By 1820 there were eight churches. State meetings began, irregularly, in 1837. In that year a church was formed in St. Louis, but it did not persist and was started again in 1842. Missouri was, from the start, a "strong state" for the Disciples.

Texas was still a part of Mexico when Collin McKinney, a devout "Christian" layman from Kentucky, came to the vicinity of Texarkana in 1824 and then moved on to what became Bowie County, where he spent the rest of a long and active life. He did not have a church there until a preacher came in 1842; but when there was a church, McKinney was a pillar of it, as he was of the republic, and then the state, of Texas. The first church in Texas was one that came in a body from Tennessee, with reinforcements from Alabama and Mississippi, in 1836, and settled at Clarksville. Lynn D'Spain and Mansil W. Matthews were the preachers who came with this church. David Crockett accompanied this caravan on part of its journey. At that time the Mexican constitution prohibited the exercise of any religion except the Roman Catholic, but the agencies of enforcement were weak, the seat of government was far away, and the revolution which made Texas an independent republic was imminent.

California had two churches, at Stockton and Santa Clara, within two years after the discovery of gold. They were established by Thomas Thompson, a Disciple preacher who went west with the forty-niners but preferred to evangelize, at his own expense, rather than to seek gold. This falls just beyond the limits of our period, the first two decades, but it illustrates the promptness with which Disciples followed the frontier. There is a report of a congregation organized in Oregon Territory in 1846, three years after the beginning of the "great immigration" and the very year in which American title to the territory was settled by treaty with England.

CAMPBELL AT HIS ZENITH

Alexander Campbell's activities during these years were constant and varied. The *Millennial Harbinger* furnished a medium for the development and expression of his ideas and for the exchange of news and opinions among the churches. His many long tours for lecturing and preaching were more fruitful in building morale and gaining publicity for the movement than in winning converts, for he was never a very effective evangelist. But from the testimony of unbiased witnesses, he must have been one of the most impressive figures that ever stood upon an American platform. Mrs. Trollope, mother of the English novelist, and herself the author of *Domestic Manners of the Americans*, was present at the debate with Owen and described Mr. Campbell as "the universal admiration of his audience."

In 1836 Mr. Campbell published a volume entitled *The Christian System*. This came near to being such an "exhibition of the fullness and precision of the Holy Scriptures upon the entire subject of Christianity" as Thomas Campbell had suggested in the Postscript to the *Declaration and Address*. Those who had felt the sting of his denunciation of creeds now shouted with glee that here at last was the "Campbellites' creed." But it was not a creed, because it was never used as a creed and was never intended to be so used. It was a rather full statement of Mr. Campbell's views on every religious topic that he considered important. But no church or organization of churches ever adopted it. No applicant for membership was ever asked to accept it. No minister's orthodoxy was ever tested by it. No one could even be required to read it. The book itself repudiates the notion of requiring conformity to this or any other body of doctrine. In it the author says:

> The belief of one fact is all that is requisite, as far as faith goes, to salvation. The belief of this one fact and submission to one institution expressive of it, is all that is required of Heaven to admission into the church. The one fact is expressed in the single proposition, that Jesus the Nazarene is the Messiah. The one institution is baptism.

The Christian System, then, was certainly not a creed, since it declared that only "one fact and one institution" were essential.

But when he placed the "one institution" on a par with the "one fact," Mr. Campbell did not mean to imply that the unimmersed could not be Christians. A lady wrote from Lunenburg, Virginia, in 1837, expressing surprise at some reference he had made to unimmersed Christians. In reply to this "Lunenburg letter," Mr. Campbell wrote a memorable article for the *Millennial Harbinger* and followed it with two even more emphatic statements answering objections. In this article, he wrote:

> Who is a Christian? I answer, Everyone that believes in his heart that Jesus of Nazareth is the Messiah, the Son of God; repents of his sins, and obeys him in all things according to his measure of knowledge of his will....

> I cannot ... make any one duty the standard of Christian state or character, not even immersion....

> * * * * * * *

> It is the image of Christ the Christian looks for and loves; and this does not consist in being exact in a few items, but in general devotion to the whole truth as far as known.

> There is no occasion, then, for making immersion, on a profession of the faith, absolutely essential to a Christian—though it may be greatly essential to his sanctification and comfort.

In answering an objection to the original article, Mr. Campbell stated:

> Now the nice point of opinion on which some brethren differ, is this: Can a person who simply, not perversely, *mistakes* the outward baptism, have the inward ... which changes his state and has praise of God, though not of all men?... To which I answer, that, in my opinion, *it is possible.*

In 1837 Mr. Campbell defended Protestantism in a debate with the Roman Catholic, Archbishop Purcell, of Cincinnati. It was a period in which there was much anti-Catholic agitation, stimulated by what the Native American party called "the rapidly increasing political influence of the papal power in the United States" and by the violently reactionary policy of the papacy against every liberal and democratic movement in Europe. The public and the press had not yet adopted the hush-hush attitude toward the Catholic question. Neither of the contestants sought this controversy. They were virtually forced into it by the public interest in lectures which both had delivered before a teachers' association in Cincinnati. The debate was held in Cincinnati. It continued through eight days and made a great impression on the city. Mr. Campbell had now defended Protestantism against the highest Roman Catholic dignitary who ever participated in such a public discussion in this country, and he had earlier defended Christianity against one of the most eminent secularists and skeptics of the time. These debates were published and widely circulated.

But for the exposition and defense of his own movement, the high point in Campbell's career as a debater was his debate with the Presbyterian minister, N. L. Rice, at Lexington, Kentucky, in 1843. Henry Clay served as moderator. The debate lasted for eighteen days. Four of the six propositions had to do with baptism. Campbell affirmed that the act is immersion and the purpose is the remission of past sins. Rice affirmed that the infant of a believing parent is a proper subject, and that baptism may be administered only by a bishop or ordained presbyter. In the other two propositions, Campbell affirmed that the Holy Spirit operates only through the Word in conversion and sanctification, and that creeds are necessarily "heretical and schismatical." This debate, published in a thick volume of more than 900 closely printed pages, became a book of reference for generations of Disciples and perhaps did as much as any other one thing to standardize their thinking and practice.

The duty of founding colleges for the education of ministers, the building of an intelligent laity, and the Christian culture of society was suggested almost as soon as the Disciples realized that they were a separate body committed to a long-term enterprise. A charter was obtained in 1833 for a college at New Albany, Indiana, but nothing came of it. The first actual college of the Disciples was Bacon College, founded at Georgetown, Kentucky, in 1836. The name was selected to honor Francis Bacon and to register approval of his empirical philosophy. Walter Scott was its first president, but he did little beyond delivering an inaugural address, and within less than a year he was succeeded by D. S. Burnet. The school was moved to Harrodsburg in 1839, was discontinued in 1850, was revived as Kentucky University, and in 1865 was moved to Lexington, where it acquired the property and historic tradition of Transylvania University.

Bethany College was incorporated in 1840 and opened soon after. Mr. Campbell projected and organized it, gave the land which became its beautiful campus, raised the money for its building and maintenance, and served as its president for more than twenty years. His writings on education, especially the series of articles in the *Millennial Harbinger* during the year when he was making his plans for Bethany, prove that he was an original and creative thinker in the field of both general and Christian education. His expectations as to the service his college would render to the movement as a whole were amply realized. It became for a time the principal training school for ministers and the educational center for the laity; and it was the "mother of colleges" among the Disciples.

CHAPTER VIII
ORGANIZATION AND TENSIONS, 1849-74

As the Disciples grew and spread, the need of organization on a national scale was felt. There were still lingering doubts as to whether fidelity to the "ancient order of things" permitted such organization. But the prevailing decision was that meetings of "deputies, messengers or representatives" of the churches might properly be held if they would remember that they are "voluntary expedients" and "have no authority to legislate in any matter of faith or moral duty" but exist only "to attend to the ways and means of successful cooperation." These words, quoted from a resolution adopted by a conference on cooperation held at Steubenville, Ohio, in 1844, express the policy that became permanent.

Mr. Campbell himself, laying aside any earlier prejudice against what he had called "popular schemes" among the denominations, urged "a more general and efficient cooperation in the Bible cause, in the missionary cause, in the educational cause." But so long as the Disciples had no agency of their own for foreign missionary work he recommended (1845) that they support the Baptist Missionary Society. And when, in the same year, D. S. Burnet and other brethren in Cincinnati organized an "American Christian Bible Society," he felt that this action was premature, that it was not sufficiently representative of the whole brotherhood, and that more could be accomplished with the available funds by contributing them to the (Baptist) American and Foreign Bible Society. He was no isolationist, and he bore no grudge against the Baptists, in spite of the acrimonies that had accompanied the expulsion of the Reformers from Baptist churches and associations a few years earlier. He also endorsed the Evangelical Alliance as soon as it was formed in 1846.

The demand for a national convention that would represent the whole body of Disciples found voice through most of the influential journals. All who urged a convention spoke of it as a meeting of "delegates" appointed by the churches. To those who still objected that conventions and missionary societies were no part of the "ancient order," Mr. Campbell replied that in such matters of method and procedure the church is "left free and unshackled by any apostolic authority."

NATIONAL ORGANIZATION

The first national convention of Disciples met at Cincinnati, October 24-28, 1849, with 156 representatives from one hundred churches in eleven states. Some came as delegates with credentials from their churches. Others represented districts. The Indiana state meeting had elected messengers. But many ministers and active laymen were present who had no formal appointment and no credentials. Since these were well-known brethren, whose standing as representative Disciples no one could deny, and whose right to an equal status with the elected delegates it would have been embarrassing to challenge, it was voted to enroll all present as members of the convention. So this first national convention, though projected as a delegate convention, became a mass meeting.

The organization of a missionary society was the principal business of the convention. The name first chosen was "Home and Foreign Missionary Society," but this was immediately changed to "American Christian Missionary Society," because "the missionary cause is one"—a truth that was rediscovered in 1919. The society's name meant that it was to be an American agency for missions throughout the world, including America. Alexander Campbell was elected its first president, and he was re-elected annually as long as he lived.

No sooner had the convention been held and the society formed than the opposition to both flared up again. Jacob Creath, Jr., who had been opposed to the convention from the beginning, wanted to have another convention to discuss the legitimacy of conventions and societies. Some others argued that "the church is the only missionary society and can admit no rivals"; but these also objected to any arrangement for united action by the churches, so that, in their view, each congregation would have to be a separate missionary society. The criticism of conventions and societies on the ground that there was no New Testament command or precedent for them did not seem to have much popular support at this time, and it soon died down. But a few years later it became a highly controversial issue, and finally a divisive one.

The first venture abroad was the Jerusalem mission, led by Dr. James T. Barclay. Even before the convention met and before the society was formed, Dr. Barclay had been pressing the cause of foreign missions upon the Disciples, had suggested Jerusalem as a field, and had offered his services. He was a man of fine culture, with a college degree from the University of Virginia and a degree in medicine from the University of Pennsylvania, and the depth of his piety equaled the ardor of his devotion to the cause. The selection of Jerusalem as the scene of the first foreign missionary effort was based chiefly on sentimental considerations. Since the gospel had first been preached "beginning at Jerusalem," it seemed fitting that the world-wide proclamation of the "gospel restored" should also begin there. Dr. Barclay and his family reached Jerusalem in February, 1851. After three and a half years of work, not entirely unfruitful but on the whole disappointing, he returned with the report that conditions did not warrant the continuance of the mission at that time.

Soon after, the society attempted to plant a mission among the Negro freedmen who had migrated to Liberia. This colony on the west coast of Africa had but recently declared its independence, which had been recognized by most of the powers—except the United States. A Negro slave, Alexander Cross, was bought, freed, educated, and sent to evangelize among his own people; but he died of fever on the coast of Liberia before he could begin his work. In 1858 J. O. Beardslee, who had been a missionary in Jamaica with another communion, became a Disciple and returned to that island under the auspices of the American Christian Missionary Society. His work produced no notable results, but it may have helped to open the fray for the more substantial work in Jamaica some years later. These three—Jerusalem, Liberia, and Jamaica—were the only foreign missionary efforts in the twenty-five years during which the society undertook to conduct both foreign and home missions, and all three were counted as failures.

GROWTH, JOURNALISM, EDUCATION

During the quarter-century to which our attention is now directed, the American Christian Missionary Society did something toward sending evangelists to neglected areas and planting churches on the frontier. State societies did more. But the work that produced the very substantial growth in this period was done chiefly by churches and evangelists acting independently, by county and neighborhood cooperation, and by individuals who were following the westward tide of migration. While churches were being established in the new Western territories and states as fast as population flowed into them, there was also a steady increase of membership in the Central states, where the movement had had its beginnings. After a tour of Indiana in 1850, Mr. Campbell reported that "our people" in that state were second only to the Methodists in numbers, resources, and influence. Their standing in Kentucky at that time was certainly no worse. Development east of the Alleghenies was relatively slow and slight, except in Virginia and North Carolina, where early visits and preaching by Disciple ministers had proved fruitful. These two states would have been even stronger if they had not lost, while the Western states were gaining, by the westward current of migration. In other Eastern states there were some notable old churches, some of which originated under Haldanean, Sandemanian, or similar influences and became affiliated with the Disciples, but they did not greatly multiply.

The total numerical growth from 1849 to 1874 was not merely substantial; it was amazing. By the middle of the nineteenth century, after twenty years of separate existence, the Disciples had about 118,000 members. In the 1850-60 decade their numbers were almost doubled to 225,000. For 1870, the figure is given as 350,000. By 1875 it was probably close to 400,000. This growth is the more remarkable because it was accomplished with very little help from promotional organizations and with very little general planning.

The abundance and vigor of the periodicals devoted to the defense of the faith and the dissemination of news of the churches did much to make up for the lack of more official agencies of cooperation. The editors had no authority, but they exercised wide influence in the spread of ideas and the promotion of acquaintance among the Disciples in scattered communities. James M. Mathes published the *Christian Record* at various places in Indiana, with some intermissions, from 1843 to 1884. By far the most influential editor, aside from Campbell and Errett, was Benjamin Franklin, a collateral relative of the famous Dr. Benj. Franklin.

Our Ben Franklin began his long and notable editorial career in 1845 with a paper which, beginning as the *Reformer* and passing through several changes and mergers, became the *American Christian Review*. He was a powerful supporter of the missionary society until, after serving as its secretary for a short time, he turned against it and became the most effective opponent of organized work. More important than this was the sledge-hammer evangelism that he carried on incessantly, with the spoken as well as the written word. Completely without formal education, he developed a clear and trenchant style which does not need his biographer's apologies. The favorite theme of his writing, and the sole theme of his preaching, was the "plan of salvation" and the plea of the Disciples for that simple gospel and the restoration of the church on the apostolic pattern. A volume of his evangelistic sermons, *The Gospel Preacher*, was the handbook for hundreds of other preachers and kept its popularity for half a century. One must know Ben Franklin, and realize how many there were like him, though built to a smaller scale, to understand how the Disciples grew so fast in this pioneer period—and why they ran into some difficulties later. Franklin also helped to save the Disciples from division over slavery and the Civil War by urging that the sole business of the church is to preach the gospel. In doing this, he also helped to fasten upon them the idea that the church must be neutral on all social and economic questions. A Christian "should make his money according to the laws of business and spend it according to the laws of God," said one eminent minister.

About 1850 there arose a great zeal for founding colleges. In several states the Disciples had become strong enough, or felt sure that they soon would be strong enough, to support a college. Schools were needed to train ministers, to provide an educated laity, to hold the loyalty of the young people of their own families and win others, and to make their fair contribution to the culture of new communities in which there was little provision for tax-supported education.

In 1845 the Disciples had three colleges: Bacon, at Harrodsburg, Kentucky; Bethany, at what is now Bethany, West Virginia; and Franklin, near Nashville, Tennessee. Within a year or two before or after 1850, at least nine colleges and institutes were established, most of which still live. These included: Kentucky Female Orphan School, Midway, Kentucky; Western Reserve Eclectic Institute, which became Hiram College, Hiram, Ohio; Northwestern Christian University, which became Butler University, Indianapolis, Indiana; Walnut Grove Academy, which grew into Eureka College, Eureka, Illinois; Christian College (for girls), Columbia, Missouri; Abington College, Abington, Illinois, which later merged with Eureka; Berea College, Jacksonville, Illinois, which died young; Arkansas College, Fayetteville, Arkansas, which met the same fate; and Oskaloosa College, Oskaloosa, Iowa, which had thirty useful years before it was dimmed by the brighter light of Drake University.

The percentage of survival in this list is unusually high. It was much lower among the colleges started during the next twenty or thirty years. The cost of maintaining a good college, according to the standards of that time, was very little in comparison with present needs, but it was more than most of the eager college founders thought it would be. Many schools were started which had not a sufficient constituency. Others were brought forth by the local pride of an optimistic young settlement and withered away when its hope was deferred or its boom collapsed—for while Chicago and Kansas City grew miraculously, many a "future metropolis" of the Middle West remained a village. Few of the new colleges were adequately financed, even for a modest beginning. The mortality rate was therefore high. The Disciples were not alone in this. Other denominations lost many infant colleges. By 1865 there was a general complaint about the reckless multiplication of weak colleges. Moses E. Lard expressed the mind of many when he wrote: "We are building ten where we should have but one. One great university, with a single well-endowed college in each state where we number fifty thousand, is sufficient."

One is rather surprised to find, running through several issues of the *Millennial Harbinger* in that same year, a discussion as to whether the Disciples needed a good theological school for the graduate training of the ministry. W. K. Pendleton, Campbell's son-in-law (twice) and his successor as president of Bethany College and as editor of the *Millennial Harbinger*, argued that there was need of a school to give ministers a professional education beyond what the colleges can or should furnish. Isaac Errett agreed with Pendleton. Ben Franklin, naturally, opposed. Nothing was done. For another thirty or forty years the Disciples continued to consider training for the ministry as a phase of undergraduate education.

"WE CAN NEVER DIVIDE"

Through these years the slavery issue was mounting to the crisis of war. All the churches were deeply stirred. Methodists, Baptists, and Presbyterians divided. Congregationalists, being practically all in the North and therefore all on the same side of the question, did not divide. The Episcopal Church peaceably divided when the country was divided by secession, and as peaceably reunited when the country was reunited. Disciples were nearly equal in numbers, North and South. They might easily have divided, but they did not.

Alexander Campbell's sentiments were against slavery and he was never a slaveholder, but he lived in a slave state and had little sympathy with radical abolitionism. Much of the patronage and financial support of Bethany College came from the South, and he tried to keep the college neutral on these controversial issues. The first graduating class of Northwestern Christian University (Butler) was made up of a group of students who withdrew from Bethany in sympathy with a young man who had been expelled for making an antislavery speech after the public discussion of that question in the college had been forbidden. Campbell had elaborated his position in a series of articles in 1845: slavery is not condemned in the New Testament; therefore holding slaves is not sinful *per se* and cannot be a ground for withdrawing Christian fellowship; masters must do their full Christian duty toward their slaves, though it is admittedly very difficult to maintain a fully Christian attitude toward a person while owning him as a slave; slavery is economically bad and morally dangerous; and the policy to be followed in any situation is a matter of "opinion" and therefore within the area of Christian liberty.

That useful distinction between faith and opinion, which was fundamental to the Disciples' program for union, now saved them from division over slavery and war. All political and social questions were to be treated as matters of opinion on which Christians might differ without dividing. Fourteen ministers in Missouri, including J. W. McGarvey, published in 1861 a "pacifist manifesto" urging Disciples to take no part in the war. They did not argue that war is always wrong or anti-Christian, nor did they discuss any moral issue of the war that was then beginning. Their whole point was that "our movement" would suffer disastrously if its members were to take arms against each other. Few Disciples were guided by their advice. Most of them, North and South, apparently felt that their attitudes in a great national crisis could not be determined by the consideration of what might happen to "our movement"—or else they thought that the movement could stand it, as it did.

The first national convention after the outbreak of war, meeting at Cincinnati in October, 1861, took a ten-minute recess so that its members, not as the convention but as a mass meeting, might pass a resolution of loyalty to the national government. Two years later the convention itself adopted a stronger resolution deploring the "attempts of armed traitors to overthrow our government." But even this produced no division. It was a Northern convention because, under war conditions, there could, of course, be no representation from the South. Southerners realized that the resolution was merely an expression of Northern opinion, which they already knew; and many Northerners soon came to feel that it was a mistake for a sectional convention bearing a national name to pass a resolution purporting to express the sentiments of all Disciples, including the half of the country which could not possibly be represented. The organizational weakness of the Disciples became a strength in maintaining unity when the slavery issue and civil war threatened division, for there was no court to rule out any church or section and no convention empowered to set up standards or to pass any resolution that would have the force of law for the churches.

"We can never divide!" shouted Moses E. Lard in his quarterly. If war could not divide us, he said, nothing ever can. But something could—and did. Disciples cannot divide through the exclusion of one element by another in control of denominational machinery, because there is no such machinery with power of exclusion. But it is possible to divide by voluntary withdrawal. If there is no power to put any church out, there is none to keep it in if it wants to go out. That is what happened some years later.

THE PERIOD OF CONTROVERSY

The issues upon which division actually occurred had already arisen before the Civil War and they were so hotly debated in the years immediately after it that 1866-75 is sometimes called "the period of controversy." The principal topics which were discussed with greater or less heat during this period were these: open or close communion; the title, "Reverend"; the "one-man system" of the pastorate; the alleged introduction of a creed; the use of the organ; and the missionary societies. Only the last two of these had any lasting importance as divisive issues. The first four merely illustrate the heightening tension between the strict constructionists and those who favored what they considered reasonable expedients to meet changed conditions.

When the Reformers were being excluded from Baptist churches and associations, they were accused of many things but not of departing from the Baptist practice of close communion. One must conclude that they had not yet departed from it. In 1828 Mr. Campbell objected to admitting the unimmersed to the Lord's Supper even occasionally, because he thought this would logically require admitting them to church membership. But the restriction upon the communion was gradually relaxed, without much talk about it, until Isaac Errett could write in 1862, when the question was debated at length in the *Millennial Harbinger*, that probably two-thirds of the churches welcomed to the Lord's Supper all who considered themselves qualified to commune. The solving text was that each should "examine himself and so let him eat," and the standard formula came to be, "We neither invite nor debar." There was, in fact, very little general controversy on this subject. In time the close communion practice disappeared so completely that most Disciples in the United States do not know that it ever existed and are somewhat shocked to learn that it still prevails in the British churches.

The presentation to Mr. Errett of a silver door plate with "Reverend" before his name precipitated a brief but lively argument. Aversion to this title had been common among the earlier restorers of primitive Christianity. The *Christian Baptist* had said many a caustic word about clerical pretensions of dignity and usurpations of power, of which "Reverend" was considered a symbol. But as Disciples came to have more and larger churches and a ministry more clearly distinguished from the laity, they became less sensitive about a title which, in practice, meant only that its bearer was a minister. The title long remained unpopular, but the issue faded out.

Protest against the "one-man system" had a similar motive but more substantial ground. The enlarging function of the pastor and the somewhat diminished prominence of the lay elders, as town and city churches with settled full-time ministers multiplied, evoked a futile resistance to the passing of those frontier conditions under which lay leadership for the churches had been successful. "Mutual edification" had been considered by many to be an essential part of the ancient order. No division came from this difference in practice and terminology, and the difference itself tended to disappear. One of the ultraconservatives gave the reason when he wrote: "Brethren, no system of edification can be scriptural if it doesn't edify."

When Mr. Errett, as minister of a new church in Detroit, issued for public information a brief "Synopsis" of the Disciples' position, there was an outcry against it as a "creed." Strangely enough, the chief critic, Moses E. Lard, had himself put forth "sixteen specifications of fundamental principles." This episode is worth noting only because it shows how keen the legalists were to find proofs that the Disciples had become degenerate and had gone off after "innovations."

NOT DIVIDED—YET

The organ question, unlike the four issues that have been mentioned, cut deep, lasted long, and contributed to division. Protestant opposition to instrumental music in public worship began with Zwingli and Calvin (who were also strict restorers of primitive Christianity) and reappeared among New England Congregational churches in the eighteenth century. It did not become important among the Disciples before 1860, because there were few organs. About that time, L. L. Pinkerton said that he was the only preacher in Kentucky who favored the use of the organ and that his church at Midway was the only church that had one. The organ in public worship was, in truth, an "innovation." The case against it was completely stated by J. W. McGarvey in the *Millennial Harbinger* for November, 1864: The organ is not merely an aid to singing, like hymnbooks or a tuning fork, or a convenient accessory to the church building, like a stove, but is a distinct and novel element in worship; no element in public worship is legitimate unless it is explicitly authorized in the New Testament; instrumental music is not so authorized; therefore it is not legitimate. The crucial question was whether the New Testament does, as he claims, undertake to specify all the permissible elements of public worship. And the answer to that question is part of the answer to the larger question as to what is to be restored in the restoration of primitive Christianity. Back of that lies the still more basic question as to the nature of the New Testament. Churches did not disfellowship each other over the organ question, but many congregations divided on it.

The most serious of all the controversies was about the missionary societies, national and state. Those who sought in the primitive church a model for all the procedures of the church, as well as a blueprint for its structure, found no justification for societies. There had been some protests when district and state meetings were first proposed and more when the national convention and missionary society were organized. This opposition had waned, but it was revived in the 1860's with new vigor and new journalistic champions. The war, the loyalty resolutions, acrimony over the organ, the failure of the society's three foreign missions, and the widening social and economic gap between the plain people of the country churches and the more sophisticated townsfolk—these all helped to bring in an era of ill will. Cultural isolation and the lack of educated leaders in this middle period favored the tendency toward a narrow legalism. The death of Alexander Campbell on March 4, 1866, after he had been president of the American Christian Missionary Society for more than sixteen years, made it possible for its opponents to dig up and reprint under his name the antisociety fulminations of the *Christian Baptist* forty years earlier. Almost at the same time Benjamin Franklin turned against the society and made his *American Christian Review* a powerful weapon of attack. The main onslaught was not against the management of the society but against the idea of having any society at all. However, all these hostile influences were the more damaging because the A.C.M.S. was not, in fact, doing much work.

To satisfy the critics and prevent the threatened disruption, a completely new plan of cooperation was devised by a committee of twenty, including both society and antisociety men. The product of its labors was the "Louisville Plan," which was adopted almost unanimously by the convention of 1869. Under this plan the A.C.M.S. ceased to function. Its place was taken by a system of general, state, and district conventions, with boards, secretaries, and treasurers springing from and reporting to the three levels of conventions. In theory, it was a closely knit fabric of delegate conventions, the General Convention being composed of delegates from the state conventions, these of delegates from district conventions, and the district conventions of messengers elected by the churches. The wonder is that the antisociety men accepted it for a moment as (Ben Franklin's words) "a simple and scriptural plan." They did not accept it long, and even the friends of the society were cool to it. "Scriptural" or not, it was incredibly cumbersome and impractical. Receipts for national missionary work fell off from about $10,000 to an average of less than $4,000 a year for the next decade. Missionary cooperation had to take a fresh start; and so it did with the beginning of the next period.

It was largely due to Isaac Errett and the *Christian Standard* that the Disciples did not become a legalistic and exclusive sect. The paper was founded at Cleveland in 1866—its first issue carried the news of Alexander Campbell's death—and it was moved to Cincinnati in 1869. Errett was already a man of power and distinction. He had been pastor, author, co-editor of the *Millennial Harbinger*, corresponding secretary of the American Christian Missionary Society, and president of the convention. In starting the *Christian Standard* he had the active support of General Garfield and three of the Phillips brothers of Newcastle, Pennsylvania. The new journal at once threw its influence boldly on the liberal side of all the controversial issues that have been mentioned. The *Gospel Advocate* already was, and the *American Christian Review* was soon to be, arrayed against all "innovations." To complicate the picture, the *Apostolic Times* was established with an impressive list of editors—Lard, Graham, Hopson, Wilkes, and McGarvey—who aimed to heal the incipient division by taking what they considered a middle-of-the-road position, against the organ but for the missionary society.

The service of Isaac Errett would have been less significant than it was if it had been only the championing of the progressive side in certain controversies. What was more important was the breadth of his spirit, the depth of his religious life, and the power of his leadership away from a cramping legalism and toward a broader spiritual culture. In an article entitled "What Is Sectarianism?" in the *Christian Quarterly*, January, 1871, Mr. Errett restated the aim of the Disciples of Christ as union upon Christ, not upon our own interpretation of the Bible or on an exact pattern of the "ancient order of things." J. J. Haley later called this article "the Declaration and Address brought down to date."

CHAPTER IX
RENAISSANCE, 1874-1909

After the dark ages of controversy and organizational stagnation—which were by no means so dark in other respects—came a renaissance in which the Disciples gained a clearer view of their central purpose and a better command of the resources for realizing it. They began to make more intimate contacts with the social and intellectual currents of the time and to escape from the cultural isolation into which they had fallen. Those who thought of this as apostasy from the true faith tended to withdraw, and ultimately did withdraw, into a separate and noncooperating group. The main body no longer took interest in what now seemed trivial disputes about organs, pastors, and the legitimacy of missionary organizations. The new issues which arose were such as were shared by the whole Christian world, so that even their dissensions related them to the main currents of religious thought.

This period saw the continuance of westward expansion, the winning of a second and almost a third half-million members, the creation of new missionary and benevolent organizations, more than a hundredfold increase in giving for missions, new journalistic enterprises, an educational awakening, a new type of evangelism, new outreaches in Christian union and interdenominational cooperation, and some slight beginning of a discovery of social ethics as a field of Christian responsibility.

The "dark ages" had not been stagnant in numerical and geographical growth. That process needed only to be continued. As the completion of the transcontinental railroads brought new land within reach for settlement, and as homesteaders invaded what had been the open range, towns sprang up throughout the West. In town and country, Disciples were there among the first, and churches were planted. After the American Christian Missionary Society was relieved of its foreign responsibilities, it could do more in promoting new work in the West. Soon the Board of Church Extension came to give first aid to the new church needing a house. It was never a log-cabin frontier west of the Mississippi (except Missouri and Arkansas), and building was a different problem from what it had been on the old timbered frontier. Even though the Disciples could draw less support from the East than some denominations, they became relatively strong in most of the Western states and very strong in some, such as Kansas and Oklahoma.

Total estimated membership in 1875 was 400,000. The official figure was 641,000 for 1890; 1,120,000 for 1900; 1,363,533 for 1910.

JOURNALISM AND MISSIONS

A new center of journalistic influence began when J. H. Garrison moved his paper, the *Christian*, from Quincy, Illinois, to St. Louis, on January 1, 1874, and organized the Christian Publishing Company. He had been on the point of moving it to Chicago, when the Great Fire of 1871 intervened. B. W. Johnson's *Evangelist*, which had lately moved from Iowa to Chicago, merged with the *Christian* in 1882 to produce the *Christian-Evangelist*. By its conservatively progressive policy, it became at once a powerful force in leading the Disciples out of the age of sterile controversy and into a wider conception of religion and more active work in its promotion. The *Christian Standard*, at Cincinnati, under Isaac Errett, was already exercising a similar influence. As long as Mr. Errett lived, the two papers worked together for the same ends. The relations between these two great editors were always intimate and affectionate. Writing from his deathbed (1888) to his brother editor, J. H. Garrison, who was his junior by twenty-two years, Mr. Errett said:

> We have been together from the beginning of this missionary work. We have stood shoulder to shoulder ... and the two most effective instrumentalities in educating our people and bringing them into active cooperation in spreading the gospel in all lands have been the *Christian-Evangelist* and the *Christian Standard*; and indeed, upon all points of doctrine and practice and expediency you and I have always worked on the same lines in perfect harmony.

A third paper, destined to hold a very prominent place in American journalism at a later date, was plodding its useful way through most of this period with a rather local constituency. This was the *Christian Oracle*, which began at Des Moines in 1884 and later moved to Chicago. In 1900 it became the *Christian Century*. For several years thereafter it reflected the liberal spirit of Herbert L. Willett, who was its editor for a time. Coming under the control and editorship of Charles Clayton Morrison in 1908, it soon began to evolve into an undenominational journal of religion.

The real awakening of the Disciples came with the rise of their interest in missions. Legalistic controversy over missionary methods had previously absorbed so much energy that little was left for missionary work. The old society had barely kept itself alive. The Louisville Plan had been a total failure. Into this vacuum came a band of devoted women, led by Mrs. C. N. Pearre, of Iowa City, who formed the Christian Woman's Board of Missions in 1874. The organizing ability and untiring energy that went into it would have made almost any enterprise a success. The regular meetings of the local auxiliaries and of Junior and Intermediate groups and the publication of the monthly *Missionary Tidings* and other literature constituted a vast program of missionary education. A system of regular dues produced a trickle of dimes which aggregated a torrent of dollars. By 1909 there were 60,000 adult members. Offerings up to that time had totaled nearly $2,500,000. Missions were conducted in Jamaica, India, Mexico, Puerto Rico, Argentina, and Liberia. There were schools in the backward Appalachian Mountain area, institutes and missions for Orientals on the West Coast, evangelists in thirty-three states, a missionary training school at Indianapolis, and "Bible chairs" at the Universities of Michigan, Virginia, Kansas, and Texas.

In 1875, almost with the founding of the women's work, came the organization of the Foreign Christian Missionary Society. Its early development was slow, and it was ten years before it had an office of its own or a full-time secretary. By 1881 its annual income had risen to $13,178. It was still sending the gospel only to Christians. It had missions in Denmark, England, France, and among the Armenians in Turkey, and was planning to send (but did not send) missionaries to Italy and Germany. An address by J. H. Garrison, at the convention at Louisville in 1881, appealing for missions to the heathen, led immediately to the establishment of Children's Day for that purpose. The foreign missionary deadlock was at last broken. Receipts of the foreign society doubled the next year, and G. L. Wharton and seven others were sent to India. Japan was entered in 1883, China in 1886, the Belgian Congo in 1897, Cuba in 1899. A. McLean was an invaluable missionary leader for many years, and an unforgettable personality.

When the American Society was permitted to devote itself wholly to American missions, its energies revived and it had an important part in the expansion that has been mentioned, as well as on the new frontier of foreign populations in the cities. In addition, it sponsored the Board of Church Extension, which at first made only small building loans to new and weak churches but later, as its resources increased, was able also to help some important city churches with their housing problems. George W. Muckley, as representative of Church Extension for nearly forty years, from 1888, linked his name inseparably with this cause.

The National Benevolent Association, 1887, grew out of a purely local impulse in St. Louis, but its work expanded from a single orphans' home in that city to a long list of institutions for children and old people in all parts of the country. This and the Board of Ministerial Relief showed that the Disciples were awakening to social responsibilities of which they had not previously taken account on a national scale. Ministerial "relief" was found to be inadequate, but it prepared the way for the more businesslike Pension Fund.

Renaissance in Education

At the beginning of this period a new birth in education was as badly needed as in organization and missions. It came, but not as promptly. The colleges had been founded largely as training schools for ministers, and they performed that function better than any other. From the Civil War to the end of the century they were poorly equipped, meagerly supported, and inadequately staffed. Since there were few high schools outside the cities, and the Disciples were 93 per cent rural in 1890, entrance requirements and academic standards were necessarily low. The young preacher who had finished the ministerial course in one of these colleges was supposed to have completed his professional education.

The educational awakening included three things: First, a few men in the 1890's, then scores and hundreds, went to the divinity schools and graduate departments of the great universities for further training after they had been graduated from the colleges of the Disciples. Second, these colleges themselves gained greater resources, raised their standards, and many of them became excellent institutions. Third, with well-trained men now available for faculties, there arose some graduate schools of sound quality in connection with a few of the Disciples' colleges. This advance proceeded slowly and on an uneven front. Some colleges became better than others, and some became better sooner. Some died because they could not meet the more rigorous demands of the modern age, including those of the standardizing and accrediting agencies; and some with small resources and low academic standards continued to render valuable service in educationally retarded areas. Most of the improvement in the colleges came after the beginning of the twentieth century. In 1897 there were forty-five educational institutions, including five "universities" and twenty-five colleges; and the total of their endowments was $1,177,000. Six years later this amount had been doubled. Thirty years after that, these doubled endowments had been multiplied by ten—and seventeen of the forty-five schools had disappeared.

The establishment of the first "Bible chair" at the University of Michigan by the Christian Woman's Board of Missions was a piece of educational pioneering which led to great developments and became the Disciples' most original contribution to American education. There was a touch of genius in the discovery of the obvious fact, hitherto apparently unnoticed, that the students in state universities, which were growing enormously, offered a constituency for religious education, and the further fact that there were more young Disciples in state schools than in their own colleges. Bible chairs were established at many other state universities, some under the auspices of state missionary societies, others under independent boards. Some developed into schools of religion in which several denominations cooperated. The one at the University of Virginia became an integral part of the university. The whole development showed that the education of the future lay leaders did not rest wholly with the Disciples' colleges, indispensable as these were, but could be promoted by using also state or other endowed institutions.

Similarly, the education of the ministry gained vastly by utilizing universities and theological seminaries maintained by others. Before 1909 there was already a beaten trail from some of the colleges to Yale Divinity School, and the numbers who traveled it later ran into the hundreds. Many went to Union Theological Seminary in New York, and others to Harvard, Princeton, Hartford, or Vanderbilt. The University of Chicago, which opened its doors in 1892, furnished a seat of learning in the Middle West and therefore nearer to the geographical center of the Disciples. Though its divinity school was at first nominally Baptist, it appealed definitely to students of all denominations and successfully sought ways of evading the restriction of its faculty to Baptists. The Disciples Divinity House was established, 1894, in affiliation with the university and its divinity school, and at once a large number of students came, many of whom were mature men already in the ministry but eager for graduate study. Through all these means, by the end of the period here under consideration, the educational average of ministers among the Disciples had been greatly raised and their intellectual horizons vastly widened. The improvement of the colleges was one of the causes and also one of the consequences of this.

HIGHER CRITICISM

The old differences of opinion about the organ and the missionary society continued, but there was no longer any interest in controversy about them. The opposing element ceased to cooperate with the "progressives" and was moving toward separation, which had become an accomplished fact, for all practical purposes, years before it was registered by the separate listing of the statistics of the "Churches of Christ" in the religious census of 1906.

New issues arose which afforded topics for lively debate in the papers, at preachers' meetings, and at the Congresses which met annually after 1899. Chief among these were higher criticism, the reception of the unimmersed, and federation. Since federation was the only one of these that called for collective action, and since it had very strong support as soon as it was proposed, it had full and frank discussion in the conventions also, as the other two questions did not.

"Higher criticism," or the study of the Bible by critical methods of historical and literary analysis, began in Europe early in the nineteenth century. By the middle of the century, controversy had grown hot, especially because the new method did not assume the inerrancy of the Bible, as the older orthodoxy did, and because some of the results of research cast doubt upon the historicity of some parts of the Bible. American scholars reacted, positively or negatively, to the higher criticism during the two decades after the Civil War. It became fairly well known by name, though not well understood, and there were some famous heresy trials. But Disciples did not become generally aware of it until the 1890's. Professor J. W. McGarvey, stalwart opponent of the new methods, began in 1893 his Biblical Criticism Department in the *Christian Standard*. With acumen and acrimony he denounced every new conclusion or theory about such things as the authorship of Deuteronomy and the latter part of Isaiah or the date of Daniel as an attack upon the faith and the work of "enemies of the Bible." This weekly page was widely read and much discussed. It gave great publicity to the subject and, by its caustic tone, its pungent personalities, and its identification of higher criticism with infidelity, added bitterness to what would in any case have been a very real divergence of opinion. "Few scholars and few students were permanently influenced by the department," says McGarvey's biographer and long-time associate, W. C. Morro.

Disciples were vitally interested in this battle of the Book, for they had always claimed to be, in a peculiar sense, a Bible people. Many of them remembered the first of Alexander Campbell's "rules of interpretation": in studying any book of the Bible, "consider first the historical circumstances of the book—the order, the title, the author, the date, the place, and the occasion of it." The young men who had been going to the Eastern universities and seminaries had become acquainted with the new methods of Bible study, which were directed to these very questions. The opening of the University of Chicago, just three months before the beginning of Professor McGarvey's antibiblical-criticism page, gave an immense impetus to this trend, for its president, Dr. W. R. Harper, was the most conspicuous exponent of these new methods in the United States, with extraordinary gifts for teaching and for publicity as well as for research. It might almost be said that it was Dr. Harper who put higher criticism on the map in the Middle West. Dr. Herbert L. Willett, who had been a student under Harper at Yale, became a colleague in his Semitic Department at Chicago and dean of the Disciples Divinity House. During several years he devoted much of his time to extension lecturing and the holding of institutes on the Bible. His popularity and success in this field were sensational. For most Disciples, Willett became the personal embodiment and symbol of the new biblical learning. He carried the flag with complete boldness, and his brilliant and winsome figure became a shining mark for the counterattack.

The papers were inevitably involved in the higher criticism controversy. The *Christian Standard's* position was never in doubt. It was against it, not only on Professor McGarvey's page, but on every other page as well. The *Christian-Evangelist* was cautiously liberal editorially. Its editor was not a technical scholar in this field, but his mind was always alert to discover new truth. He was hospitable to the critical methods and was not alarmed by their results, even though he did not personally accept all of them. For several years he had Dr. Willett write for the paper the weekly article on the Sunday school lesson. This showed editorial courage, rather than caution, but it was part of a consistent editorial policy that did as much as a university could have done for the education of the Disciples.

RETHINKING BAPTISM

"Open membership" had few advocates during the period under consideration, but there had already begun to be lively discussion of baptism in relation to the problem of union. When Thomas Campbell wrote the *Declaration and Address*—the event marked by the 1909 centennial as the beginning of the Disciples—he had not yet adopted the immersion of believers as part of the basis of union and communion. But after that practice was adopted by the Brush Run Church, it became an integral part of the program of the Campbells and it was a pivotal point in Scott's technique of evangelism. The "Christians" in Kentucky generally practiced immersion but considered it a matter of opinion and did not insist upon it. Those who merged with the Disciples yielded on this point and became strict immersionists. Campbell's reply to the "Lunenburg letter" showed that he regarded the pious unimmersed as Christians. Later developments showed that he would also commune with them as Christians. But he would not have favored admitting them as members, even if such a proposal had been made.

The first Disciple to argue for the admission of the unimmersed was Dr. L. L. Pinkerton, in 1868. Pinkerton, a medical doctor as well as a preacher, was a remarkably free spirit and may be called the first thorough "liberal" among the Disciples. He also challenged the theory of the inerrancy of the Bible, though he probably never heard of the higher criticism. Apparently no other Disciple of his time shared his views about either baptism or the Bible, except John Shackleford, co-editor with him of the *Independent Monthly*, a breezy magazine which lived less than two years.

W. T. Moore, a missionary in England for the Foreign Christian Missionary Society, about 1885 became minister of West London Tabernacle, an independent church having many unimmersed members. Defending himself against criticism in a convention to which he was reporting during a visit back home, he suggested that baptism might cease to be a barrier to union if it were agreed to recognize as baptized persons those who had already been sprinkled, whether as infants or as adults, but to practice only immersion thenceforth. In spite of the high regard in which he was held, this opportunistic proposal found little favor. At the Congress of Disciples in 1901, Dr. Moore renewed and elaborated this proposal, that a united church be formed at once with all Christians as members and that only immersion should be practiced thereafter.

Robert L. Cave, an eloquent Virginian, who was pastor of Central Christian Church, St. Louis, in 1889 issued a pronunciamento widely at variance with the generally accepted views of Disciples, and of other evangelical Christians, on many points and demanded a vote of confidence on that basis. Failing to get it, he withdrew, followed by nearly half of the members, and established the Non-Sectarian Church. This was the outstanding heresy case of the period. But Dr. Cave's rather casual treatment of baptism was such a small item in the sum of his heresies that it was scarcely noticed, and the whole episode produced a conservative reaction even in the minds of moderately progressive leaders. The editor of the *Christian-Evangelist* at once launched a doctrinal revival, the permanent record of which is the volume entitled, *The Old Faith Restated*. Dr. Cave's advocacy did more to retard than to advance the acceptance of liberal ideas, including ideas about baptism.

In the 1890's the religious papers began to print contributions discussing the function of baptism and questioning whether it is indispensable. R. T. Matthews, a professor at Drake, said that some of the unimmersed "are in essential union with Christ." John Shackleford denied McGarvey's statement, in the first edition of his *Commentary on Acts*, that "faith without immersion is dead." J. J. Haley, when pressed to declare categorically whether he thought baptism necessary, gave the Delphic answer that baptism is "as necessary as an ordinance can be, *considering what an ordinance is*." Thomas Munnell, former missionary secretary and one of the most honored veterans, wrote a long article, in the *New Christian Quarterly*, April, 1894, arguing that the requirement of baptism be waived in the interest of union. In the correspondence columns of the weeklies, there were expressions of the opinion that a Christian union movement which excludes from its churches a large proportion of those whom it regards as Christians is both illogical and futile. These were the opinions of a small minority, and there were vigorous replies. In 1901 Dr. H.

L. Willett published a little book, *Our Plea for Union and the Present Crisis*, which was a bold argument for open membership.

Along with much discussion, there was some action, but only a little within this period. J. M. Philputt was minister of a church on 119th St., New York, which from about 1890 to 1900 received the unimmersed as "members of the congregation," not of the church. "We receive them," he explained, "not as Disciples of Christ but simply as Christians." This distinction proved embarrassing. The practice drew too much criticism and it was abandoned. Similar "associate membership" arrangements were practiced for some time at South Broadway, Denver (B. B. Tyler); at Central, Denver (W. B. Craig); at Shelbyville, Kentucky; and elsewhere. At Hyde Park, Chicago (now University Church of Disciples of Christ), Dr. E. S. Ames in 1903 led the church into receiving unimmersed persons as "members of the congregation." Though the distinction between the two classes of members seldom came to attention it was not formally abolished until 1919 when the church became, *de jure* as well as *de facto*, an open-membership church. Long before that, in 1906, the Monroe Street Church, Chicago, of which Charles C. Morrison was pastor, had become the first church among the Disciples to receive into full membership the unimmersed members of other evangelical churches. When Morrison took over the *Christian Century* in 1908, he promptly made it an outspoken champion of liberal views, including open membership.

As the last item in the record of changing views on baptism within this period, it may be noted that at the Centennial Convention at Pittsburgh, 1909, Dr. S. H. Church, a grandson of Walter Scott, delivered an address in which he held that baptism is a matter of opinion in regard to which there should be individual liberty.

FEDERATION

The movement for federation among the Protestant denominations quickly won the favor of all Disciples except the most rigidly noncooperative, but these were many, and their voices were loud. The impulse to federation came from the new sense of the social responsibilities of the churches which became acute in the latter part of the nineteenth century. It was first proposed by the Presbyterian General Assembly as a means of getting some united action by Protestants without compromising their denominational differences and independence. After a decade of desultory discussion and some local organizations, a national Federation of Churches and Christian Workers was formed in 1901. The next year this body proposed a conference of official representatives of denominations to consider the feasibility of a federation of the denominations as such. It was at this point that the matter came before the Disciples through a brief speech by the secretary, Dr. E. B. Sanford, at the Omaha convention in 1902, following an eloquent address on Christian union by E. L. Powell. A resolution of approval was introduced by J. H. Garrison, who supposed—naïvely, as he afterward said—that it would be adopted unanimously. J. A. Lord, editor of the *Christian Standard*, objected that joining such an association would be "recognizing the denominations." The resolution was adopted, with only a small opposing vote. But the war was on, with the two papers already ranged on opposite sides. For the next four or five years, federation was the hot spot of controversy in conventions, ministers' meetings, and the press. The Disciples were represented, however, at the Interchurch Conference on Federation, at Carnegie Hall, New York City, in November, 1905, where a constitution was drafted. A mass meeting called during the Norfolk convention in 1907 approved the constitution, with only one dissenting voice, and elected representatives in the Federal Council of the Churches of Christ in America. The first meeting of the Federal Council was held at Philadelphia, February 2, 1908.

Thus the Disciples were in the Federal Council from its beginning. They also cooperated from the start with the Foreign Missions Conference of North America (1907) and the Home Missions Council (1908). Union as an objective had not been forgotten; but, while there were barriers to immediate union, cooperation with other Christians in the promotion of practical Christian ends had come to seem, to the great body of Disciples, both safe and wise.

The completion of the first hundred years was celebrated by a Centennial Convention, at Pittsburgh, October, 1909. This was a gathering of unprecedented and still unequaled size. It quickened the interest of Disciples in their own history and heritage. Coming so soon after they had embarked upon these large ventures in cooperation, it directed their minds not only to the numerical and institutional success of their own movement but also to the path of common service and the hope of unity that lay ahead. It was a true instinct that directed the choice of the centennial of the *Declaration and Address* for this observance rather than, for example, the promulgation of Walter Scott's "uniform, authoritative method of proclaiming the gospel," or the dissolution of the Mahoning Association. This choice expressed the feeling that the essence of the movement is not in its separateness or in its "particular ecclesiastical order," but in its call for union upon the will to do the will of Christ.

CHAPTER X
GROWING INTO MATURITY, 1909-45

Growth in numbers had been very rapid during the first eighty years. It was not unusual to hear the confident prediction that at this rate they would soon "take the country," and it seemed disloyalty to doubt that the rate of increase would continue. But the population of the country was also growing very rapidly, though not so rapidly as the Disciples. So long as there was an open frontier—that is, until about 1890—and even later, while the heavy westward migration continued, the Disciples outran the general population increase. But so also did the Methodists and Baptists. Immigration from Europe brought tremendous reinforcements to Roman Catholics and Lutherans, none to Disciples; and Disciples gained by conversion almost none of these immigrants or their children. The nation was becoming increasingly urban, while the Disciples remained more rural than other large communions. Inevitably there were diminishing returns in growth.

There was a high point in 1910. It was higher still in 1914, with an abrupt drop of nearly 300,000 to 1915, and a fair rate of growth thereafter. An improvement in statistical methods probably explains the greater part, though perhaps not all, of the apparent loss in 1915. Certainly there was no great disastrous event in that year. Perhaps some of the "Churches of Christ" were included in the count until 1915. Here are the figures since 1900:

1900	1,120,000
1905	1,238,515
1910	1,363,533
1915	1,142,206
1920	1,178,079
1925	1,450,681
1930	1,554,678
1935	1,618,852
1940	1,669,222
1944	1,681,933

Improving the Machinery

With the recognition of many fields of responsibility besides home and foreign missions and the consequent multiplication of societies, each having an annual "special day" to promote its work and raise its funds, a good deal of rivalry and confusion ensued. There were not enough days to go around. For example, the Foreign Society bitterly opposed the claim of the new American Christian Education Society (1903) upon the third Sunday in January as Education Day, because this interfered with the exclusive occupancy of January and February in preparation for Foreign Missions Day, the first Sunday in March; but it could do nothing about it because the latter was an independent and theoretically coordinate society. Moreover, the conventions were conventions of the societies rather than of the churches.

The first step toward remedying this condition was the appointment of a "calendar committee," at Buffalo in 1906, to devise a plan for reducing the number of special days. There was no immediate result. At New Orleans in 1908, the constitution of the American Christian Missionary Society was amended to provide for a delegate convention in which every church, whether contributing or not, should have elected representatives. So much parliamentary confusion attended this action that it was not carried into effect. The Centennial Convention of 1909 appointed a standing committee to consider unifying all missionary and philanthropic work under one or two boards. The committee's intimation that it would recommend a strictly delegate convention to which all societies should report touched off a long and heated discussion. "Delegate convention" became, for the more conservative element, a symbol of apostasy, as "higher criticism" and "federation" had been a few years earlier.

The formal report of the committee was made at Louisville in 1912, and the vote was almost unanimous in favor of a general convention to be composed of elected and accredited delegates from the churches. The convention of the following year, at Toronto—which was supposed to be composed of delegates but was not, because few churches sent them—ratified the delegate plan which it failed to exemplify. In subsequent conventions also there were few delegates. The delegate system failed not because of opposition but because of indifference to it. The vast majority of churches did not elect delegates, and habitual convention-goers continued to go whether they were delegates or not. At Kansas City, 1917, a new constitution was adopted, which, while retaining the delegate feature, made it meaningless by giving equal voting power to all members of churches who were in attendance. (It was like having an elected Congress with the provision that any citizen who cares to attend its sessions shall have all the powers of a congressman.) But with a large and representative "Committee on Recommendations" serving as an upper house, the plan works surprisingly well.

A national publication society, to be owned by the brotherhood and operated for its benefit, seemed desirable to many. A committee was appointed in 1907 to study the problem. Mr. R. A. Long solved it by agreeing, in December, 1909, to buy all the stock of the Christian Publishing Company, publishers of the *Christian-Evangelist* and of books and Sunday school materials, and place it in the hands of a self-perpetuating board of directors, all profits to be appropriated to the missionary and other enterprises of the Disciples. The fears of a regimentation of opinion by an "official" journal and publishing house have proved groundless. The Christian Board of Publication is, in fact, no more "official" than are the Disciples' colleges, which have exactly the same kind of ownership and control. But the brotherhood does get the profits, which have totaled much more than Mr. Long's original gift.

Mr. Long was also the prime mover in, and the largest donor to, the Men and Millions Movement, the aim of which was to enlist a thousand men and women for religious service and to raise six million dollars for missions and colleges. The campaign, beginning in 1914, was interrupted by the war, but its financial goal was finally reached.

The unification of missionary agencies had been suggested at least as early as 1892 and discussed at intervals thereafter. Before it was accomplished, the separate societies had already reformed some of the evils of the old system by establishing a joint budget committee to make the securing of funds for the various interests cooperative rather than competitive, and by stressing weekly giving for missions as part of each congregation's financial system instead of relying upon spasms of appeal on special days. Conditions caused by World War I doubtless precipitated the consolidation of the societies. In 1919 the home and foreign missionary societies, the Christian Woman's Board of Missions, the boards of church extension and ministerial relief, and the National Benevolent Association were merged to form the United

Christian Missionary Society. F. W. Burnham was its president until 1929.

Some Disciples, without being opposed to societies on principle, had long been critical of much that the societies did and the way they did it—their "cold institutionalism" and "bureaucratic methods" and their concern with so many things other than winning converts by the simple plea of faith, repentance, and baptism and organizing churches according to the ancient order. The United Society fell heir to these hostilities and aroused more. One result was an increase in the number of "independent agencies." These have a loose bond among themselves as the "Associated Free Agencies." The *Christian Standard*, chief journalistic critic of the organized work, publicizes these agencies and, together with the Christian Restoration Association, lends them its support. The annual North American Christian Convention appeals primarily to those who stand aloof from the United Society and support the independent agencies.

WIDENING EDUCATIONAL HORIZONS

The remarkable improvement of the Disciples' colleges has been an indication of the widening intellectual outlook of the communion and also one of the causes of it. The increase of endowments was only one aspect of the improvement, but an essential one. In the first thirty years of this century, the total of their endowments rose from $3,300,000 to $33,000,000. There was similar betterment of buildings, libraries, and equipment. Academic standards were raised, and faculties were better trained for their specific tasks. The transformation of Bethany College, beginning with the administration of President T. A. Cramblet, from the decadent and moribund state into which it had fallen to its present admirable and flourishing condition, is an example of what several colleges achieved. Drake, Butler, Phillips, and Texas Christian University gained honorable prominence in their states and beyond. These four developed graduate schools for the ministry, or raised toward full graduate status the departments they already had. The College of the Bible, at Lexington, entered upon a new epoch. Transylvania, always prominent in Kentucky, resumed the ancient name which identified it as "the oldest college west of the Alleghenies." There were also casualties among the colleges. As costs increased and academic requirements stiffened, some were forced to close down. Cotner was one of these.

Meanwhile, much larger numbers of the younger ministers have been taking advantage of the resources of other universities and seminaries. Hundreds have gone to Yale Divinity School, hundreds more to the Divinity School of the University of Chicago and the Disciples Divinity House. The pastors of the great majority of the larger churches at the present time are men who have had such education. Likewise the faculties of the Disciples' colleges and of their graduate schools for the ministry are composed, almost without exception, of university-trained men. The "cultural isolation" of the Disciples has definitely ended.

The Congresses of the Disciples, which began in 1899 and were held annually until about 1925, were a valuable means of adult education for ministers. These were gatherings for the discussion of religious, theological, and social problems which could not properly come before the conventions. They were characterized by great freedom of utterance. At first, all phases of opinion were represented, but as the more conservative element gradually dropped out, the congresses lost much of their value.

LIBERAL TENDENCIES

Through all these agencies, the liberalizing effects of the newer learning were widely diffused. One aspect of this was that a great number of ministers accepted the so-called "modern view" of the Bible, based upon historical and critical methods of study, in place of the theory of inerrancy and level inspiration. Proof texts lost something of their finality. The pattern of the primitive church seemed somewhat less sharply drawn, and the duty of restoring it in every detail less axiomatic. Christian truth and duty were seen as far more extensive, and far less simple, than the conversion formula and the restoration of the ancient order as these had been conceived. In this atmosphere of opinion, the stress was upon union, while the concept of restoration seemed to require reinterpretation to give it continued validity. All this had begun to happen in the previous period; but now it happened on a large scale, reaching many important pulpits, the colleges, the missionary executives, the missionaries themselves.

It was no longer possible to say that only a little coterie of young men held and taught these disturbing ideas. Their spread could not plausibly be charged to the Campbell Institute, though this provided a free forum for its members. The Campbell Institute began in 1896 as a company of fifteen young men who had done some graduate work, or were still doing it. It was organized, as its constitution says, "to enable its members to help each other to a riper scholarship by a free discussion of vital problems; to promote quiet self-culture and the development of a higher spirituality both among the members and among the churches with which they shall come in contact; and to encourage productive work with a view of making contributions of permanent value to the literature and thought of the Disciples of Christ." The young men grew older, and their number increased to several hundred. The institute's meetings were all open to the public, its membership was opened to any college graduate who cared to enroll, and a wide variety of theological opinions found expression on its programs and in its organ, the *Scroll*. It never pulled a wire to get one of its members into a position of honor or leadership. Still, it was and is of some significance as an incentive to untrammeled thinking, an organization liberal enough to be equally hospitable to liberal and conservative opinion.

The *Christian Century*, immediately after C. C. Morrison became its proprietor and editor in 1908, became the exponent of a more liberal theology than had ever been voiced by any Disciples' paper, an equally liberal social outlook, and the strongest possible emphasis upon the unity of all Christians. Gradually, and quite definitely from about 1920, it became an undenominational journal with a large constituency among all communions. The prestige that it gained in the wider field and its complete editorial independence gave it great influence among thoughtful Disciples as a stimulus to their own thinking even if they did not go all the way with it.

The Association for the Promotion of Christian Unity, which grew out of a meeting called by Peter Ainslie at the 1910 Topeka convention, of which he was president, stressed the things which the Disciples held in common with other communions and, through many years, sought ways of cultivating this fellowship. While the association itself did not espouse open membership, it did not envision union by the universal acceptance of the Disciples' "historic plea" for the immersion of penitent believers for the remission of sins and the restoration of the pattern of the New Testament church as they had understood it. But Dr. Ainslie, who was president of the association for many years, became an outspoken advocate of open membership, which he called "recognizing the equality of all Christians before God."

Missionaries in certain foreign fields, especially China, were reported to be too little concerned with baptizing converts and too much involved in activities other than pressing the "distinctive plea" of the Disciples. Whether or not they actually received Chinese Methodists or Presbyterians who had no other church home, remained a disputed question even after a self-appointed investigator had gone to China and reported that they did.

CONSERVATIVE REACTION

From all these circumstances there arose a vigorous campaign of criticism against all the agencies that seemed implicated in this liberal tendency. The attack upon Transylvania University and the College of the Bible, long a citadel of orthodoxy but now manned by younger men of university training, was spearheaded by the Bible College League in 1916. It failed to accomplish its purpose. The "Medbury resolution," passed by the 1918 convention, demanded that the Foreign Society forbid the reception of unimmersed persons into mission churches in China. An explanation by Frank Garrett that what looked from a distance like open membership in China was really not that, because the mission communities were not fully organized churches, brought the repeal of the Medbury resolution.

But criticism was only checked, not silenced. The "restorationists" organized the New Testament Tract Society to spread "sound doctrine." The Board of Managers of the new United Society adopted an affirmation of allegiance to the "historic position" of the Disciples, including immersion, signed it themselves, and required all missionaries to sign it. The 1922 convention adopted the "Sweeney resolution," which approved this action and put teeth into it. A "peace committee," in 1924, failed to agree, and the *Christian Standard* led in organizing the Christian Restoration Association and began to publish the *Restoration Herald*. The Oklahoma City convention of 1925 adopted a resolution by which it ordered the recall of any missionary who "has committed himself to belief in the reception of unimmersed persons into church membership," and voted to send a commission to the Orient to find the facts. The commission reported that it found no open membership in China, and the Board of Managers officially interpreted the Oklahoma City resolution as "not intended to invade the right of private judgment, but only to apply to such an open agitation as would prove divisive." The critics repudiated both the report and the interpretation and, when defeated in the 1926 Memphis convention, called the first "North American Christian Convention" for October, 1927. This convention, repeated annually, has continued to be the rallying place of the opponents of the United Society.

While open membership has been thrust into the foreground in the controversy between the United Society and its critics, the society does not avow sympathy with that practice and refuses to admit that this is the real issue. But it cannot be doubted that there are two contrasting views as to the basis of the Christian unity which Disciples seek and the nature and scope of the restoration at which they aim. Under this difference lie two views of the Bible, and from it flow differences of emphasis upon baptism. The admission of the unimmersed is openly defended by relatively few, but quietly practiced by a good many. Still more are restrained from it, not by their own convictions, but by the feeling that at present it would promote division rather than unity.

An Ecumenical Outlook

All Protestantism has been seeking ways of cooperation and dreaming of unity during the past forty years. In these efforts the Disciples have had their full share, and their hope of unity has been more than a dream. The revived conception of an ecumenical church is congenial to their best tradition and has stirred them to reconsider the ways in which they may help in its realization.

The Federal Council of the Churches of Christ in America has been the foremost cooperative agency since 1905. A Disciple suggested that name, and Disciples had a part in its organization and have been well represented in its leadership. Jesse Bader has been at the head of its department of evangelism for many years. Herbert L. Willett was in charge of its Midwestern office for a considerable period. Edgar DeWitt Jones has served as its president. The Disciples have entered heartily into cooperative educational work in foreign missions and into comity arrangements both at home and abroad for the allotment of fields and the distribution of forces to prevent duplication and competition. A Disciple missionary, Samuel Guy Inman, has been the leading spirit in the Committee on Cooperation in Latin America. The Interchurch World Movement, which aimed at a revival of Christian work and the strengthening of all Christian institutions immediately after World War I, was overambitious and became a costly fiasco. Disciples shared in this, too, and paid their part of the staggering deficit.

What is more explicitly called the Ecumenical Movement began with a World Conference on Foreign Missions, at New York City in 1900. This led to a similar conference in Edinburgh in 1910. The Disciples were not represented in the organization or on the program of either of these. In the minds of the promoters of these conferences, they were still an unknown people, or a minor sect. Some Disciples attended, however, as unofficial observers. Beginning with the problem of unity in missions, the Ecumenical Movement expanded to become "Life and Work" (Stockholm, 1925, and Oxford, 1937) and "Faith and Order" (Lausanne, 1927, and Edinburgh, 1937). The problems of Christianity in relation to other world religions were studied at the Jerusalem Conference, 1930, and those of the "younger churches" of the mission lands at Madras, 1939. In all these ecumenical gatherings, the Disciples have had a recognized place and have taken an active part. They have also recorded their adherence to the World Council of Churches, which grew out of the Oxford and Edinburgh conferences of 1937.

Sunday school work had an undenominational aspect at its very beginning, early in the nineteenth century. Disciples took part in the International Sunday School Association, organized in 1872, and adopted its uniform lessons. B. B. Tyler was its president in 1902. Other organizations arose to develop more modern phases of religious education. Robert M. Hopkins was prominent in the Sunday School Council from the start, and he was chairman of the executive committee of the International Council of Religious Education for eleven years after its formation by the union of the old International Association and the Sunday School Council in 1922. Roy G. Ross is now executive secretary of the International Council. Many other Disciples, experts in various phases of this work, have borne heavy responsibilities in these organizations, especially in the latest and most comprehensive one.

In brief, no communion has been more active in all the cooperative enterprises of the churches in recent years, or more sympathetic with the ecumenical trend toward thinking less of the churches and more of the Church.

The bitter experiences of World War II have accentuated the common responsibilities of all the churches in the face of a resurgent paganism and world-wide suffering. Disciples have participated in the counsels of Christians on the problems of war and peace and have not shunned their special burdens. They raised a million-dollar emergency fund, furnished their quota of chaplains with the armed forces, made provision for their conscientious objectors. The Drake Conference on "The Church and the New World Mind" was part of their contribution to the study of postwar problems.

RETHINKING THE DISCIPLES

The central body of opinion among Disciples cherishes the watchwords "union" and "restoration," about which the whole movement has developed. But it recognizes that changed conditions and widened horizons may require a reconsideration of the program of union and of the meaning of restoration. It is not the impatience of youth but the voice of experience that rejects a static and unchangeable system. J. H. Garrison was editor and editor emeritus of the *Christian-Evangelist* for sixty years. In the last contribution written with his own hand, published on April 11, 1929, being then in his eighty-eighth year, he wrote:

> Are we Disciples, who started out a century ago to plead for Christian unity, losing our zeal for this holy cause, or are we losing confidence in ourselves as fit instruments of our Lord for promoting it? I think it would be a good move for the president of our international convention to appoint at once a committee to study and report on the question: What changes in the way of addition or subtraction are demanded among the Disciples to make their plea more efficient, either in its substance or in the manner of its presentation to the world?
>
> The religious world today is very different from what it was a century ago. Science has given us a different conception of nature and of the universe. Biblical criticism has changed for most of us our view of the Bible, making it not a less but a more valuable book for the student of religion. This increase of light is evident in every department of knowledge. Is it possible that all these changes do not require any readjustment in the matter and method of a plea for unity inaugurated more than a century ago?

This suggestion bore fruit, a few years later, in the appointment of a Commission on Restudy of the Disciples of Christ. Since 1935, this commission has carried on a study of the past and the present with a view to finding what readjustments may profitably be made for the future. This is only one of many groups which are concerned that the Disciples shall not simply be "a great people," as they sometimes proudly and truly claim that they are, but shall go forward to the fulfillment of their highest purposes. There is yet much light to break from God's Word and from the teachings of their own experience.
